83921   DS
885
Allen   A63

Japan: the years of triumph

Date Due

MAR 23 '79			
NOV 3 0 78			
OCT 28 82			
MAY 12 86			
NOV 1 1988			
JAN 3 1 1989			
FEB 0 7 1990			
SEP 2 3 2002			

**CHABOT
COLLEGE
LIBRARY**

25555 Hesperian Boulevard
Hayward, CA 94545

Contents

Cover: An Italian wartime postcard
depicts a *samurai*-style figure
smashing the Pacific navies of the
USA and Great Britain
Front endpaper: A Japanese ambassador
of the 1870s in the traditional costume
of the *samurai*
Rear endpaper: Japanese troops on
a British gun emplacement in Hong
Kong cheer the news of the garrison's
surrender

Copyright © 1971: Louis Allen
First published 1971 by BPC Unit 75
St Giles House 49 Poland St London W1
in the British Commonwealth and
American Heritage Press
551 Fifth Avenue New York NY 10017
in the United States of America
Library of Congress Catalogue Card
Number: 72-134603
Made and printed in Great Britain by
Purnell & Sons Ltd Paulton Somerset

JAPAN: THE YEARS OF TRIUMPH

From feudal isolation
to Pacific empire

Louis Allen

American Heritage Press
General Editor: John Roberts

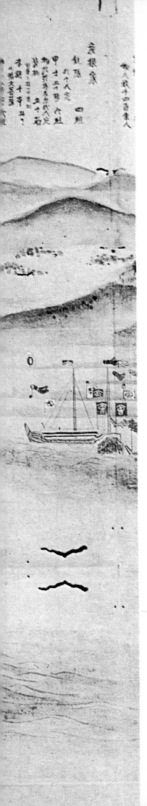

Introduction:
Entry of the West

'Great and good friend,' the letter began, 'I send you this public letter by Commodore Matthew C. Perry, an officer of the highest rank in the navy of the USA, and commander of the squadron now visiting Your Imperial Majesty's dominions . . . I have no other object in sending him to Japan but to propose to Your Imperial Majesty that the United States and Japan should live in friendship and have commercial intercourse with each other.' The letter, addressed to the Emperor of Japan by Millard Fillmore, President of the USA, went on to describe the wealth of America, and emphasised that it now took only eighteen days to go from California to Japan by steamship. Its terms were peaceful enough, but it had been far from easy to obtain an interview to deliver it, and Perry had taken the precaution of having his ships' decks cleared for action in case the Japanese dignitaries who received him changed their minds and tried to force him out. He need not have feared. Everything went well for Perry on that sunny Thursday, 14th July 1853, in Uraga Bay. For the Japanese it was a mixed blessing. Although Perry was fully conscious of the manifest destiny that had brought him at last to the approaches to the *shōgun*'s city of Edo (now Tokyo), he may not have realised how fateful his black ships were for the nation upon which he had thrust his country's commerce.

Japan had been closed to foreigners for two and a half centuries. With the exception of the tiny island of Deshima, off Nagasaki, where the Dutch were allowed to retain a trading foothold, the Seclusion Decrees of 1638 forbade Europeans to enter Japan, and threatened with death any Japanese who left their country. The reasons were partly religious, partly political. The first Europeans to visit Japan were the Portuguese, who landed on the island of Tanegashima in 1542. Seven years later, the Jesuit missionary Francis Xavier arrived in Japan ('they are the delight of my heart,' he later wrote about its people) and the Christian religion made many converts

Left: *The ending of Japan's centuries-long isolation – Matthew Perry's squadron of 'black ships' steams into Uraga Bay, 1853*

—estimated at half a million by 1614. But Dutch and English traders hinted to the *shōgun,* the hereditary military dictator and *de facto* ruler of Japan, that missionaries from Spain and Portugal were really forerunners of an attempt to seize the country. As a result, the *shōgun* persecuted the Christians and after the ruthless suppression of the last Christian rebellion at Shimabara in 1637, closed Japan to the outside world.

The *shōgun's* family, the Tokugawa, had achieved a unified feudal rule over the rest of Japan by 1615—the battle of Sekigahara in 1600 (the Culloden of Japanese history) had effectively put paid to resistance by other feudal lords. The Emperor still reigned in Kyoto, but did not govern, and his court, shorn of real power, remained an elegant ritualistic fiction of past glories in the ancient capital. The *shōgun* ruled with ruthless severity. Feudal lords whose loyalty was suspect had to reside in the shogunate capital of Edo or leave wife and children there as hostages for good behaviour. Crippling taxes left the peasantry with 'enough to live, but not enough to thrive'. And the people's loyalty was verified by compulsory registration at Buddhist temples in each neighbourhood. The Tokugawa shogunate, known as the *bakufu,* on the other hand did bring peace to Japan after a century of destructive civil wars. The large castle cities of Edo and Ōsaka became prosperous and, despite the lack of external trade, developed a flourishing economic and cultural life of their own. But this meant that the *samurai,* the military backbone of the rigidly hierarchical feudal society, lacked their obvious employment, and many of them became 'wandering soldiers' *(rōnin)* unfit for anything but oppressing the peasantry. Others profited from the education given in the feudal schools by learning Dutch and those sciences, such as European medicine, that a knowledge of Dutch made possible.

It became increasingly clear by the end of the 18th century that the *bakufu* was going to find it difficult to maintain its policy of seclusion. Russian and English ships had already tried to land at Japanese ports, sometimes to return Japanese castaways, sometimes in an attempt to trade. Russia had already begun to cast eyes on the northernmost island of Yezo (the present Hokkaidō), having established herself as a power in the Pacific: until 1867 she owned not merely a good stretch of its Asian shores, but also Alaska, including the strip of

Far left: *Perry's return visit in 1854 secured the first concessions, and created much amazement—American marines admire the girth of a Japanese* sumo *wrestler* **(top)**, *Perry and his Negro flag-bearer portrayed by a Japanese artist* **(bottom)**. **Left:** *The Ainu, a race of hunters and fishermen, were possibly the original inhabitants of Japan. A few still survive on Hokkaidō*

territory which reached halfway down to Vancouver. An American ship had been refused entry into Uraga Bay in 1845, since Japan's only official contact with the West was through Nagasaki. The *bakufu*'s inability to withstand repeated visits by strong European naval squadrons roused to fury those clans of the south-west which had been defeated in the 17th century by the Tokugawa, but still remained rich and powerful. They resented the intrusion of the foreign barbarians, and occasionally — to their cost — answered with fire from shore batteries, which the European ships soon reduced to silence: the British navy bombarded Kagoshima (chief city of the Satsuma fief) in 1862.

Samurai from these fiefs began to conspire with the court nobles from Kyoto, nostalgic for the power their families had exercised in medieval times. The movement to 'expel the foreigners' *(Jōi)* was linked with the movement to restore the Emperor to power *(Sonnō* – 'revere the Emperor') and in 1868, when the Emperor Mutsuhito (later known by his reign-name as Meiji) was fifteen, a combined attack by the Kyoto nobility and the armies of the southern clans — Satsuma, Chōshū, Hizen, Tosa — displaced the last Tokugawa *shōgun* and restored Imperial rule.

It soon became evident that one plank of the Restoration policy would have to go: *Jōi*, the expulsion of foreigners, was impracticable in an age when the West's material power was so manifest. The aim of the new rulers — equality with the Western powers who had so rudely forced open the doors of a secluded Japan — governed Japanese policy for the rest of the 19th century.

The *bakufu* had been forced to sign with the West what were termed unequal treaties, by which European and American subjects were exempt from Japanese laws and, if involved in crime, were judged by their own consuls on Japanese territory. Partly to negotiate the revision of these treaties, partly to examine Western industrial, commercial, financial, and political systems, a great embassy left Japan in 1871 to tour the USA and Europe. It was headed by a prince from the old court nobility, Iwakura, and contained many members of the new government, some with young children to be educated overseas, and *samurai* from the southern fiefs who were the new executives of Japanese power, men like Okubo Toshimichi of Satsuma and Itō Hirobumi of Chōshū. In his earlier days as a young *samurai,* Itō had watched with unalloyed pleasure his friends' destruction by fire of

Top right: The shōgun's *embassy returning from America in 1860, watched over by the souls of his ancestors. Failure to resist foreign demands spelt the end of the shogunate.* Bottom: *Leaders of the Meiji Restoration mix with the giants of the past*

the British Legation in Edo. Now, after a journey before the mast to London, Itō realised that only absorption of Western knowledge could save Japan from the fate of India and China—becoming a dependency of Britain, or finishing as a decaying empire to be divided up among whatever Western powers chose to take a piece of her.

The embassy was received in Washington by President Grant, at Windsor by Queen Victoria, by Thiers in Paris. But one visit remained in Itō's mind: in March 1873 Bismark was their host in Berlin, and told them in no uncertain terms that Japan, like Germany, would be saved by her own power. International law was a convention for normal times.

When the embassy returned to Japan it found the country in an uproar. Korea, which had co-existed uneasily with Japan for hundreds of years, had, it was claimed, treated the Japanese envoy with contumely. Ōkubo's boyhood friend, Saigō Takamori—they had been young Satsuma *samurai* together—insisted on being sent to Korea as ambassador, where he was sure the Koreans would kill him. This would provide Japan with a pretext to go to war and teach the Koreans a lesson. Ōkubo and Iwakura knew if Japan did this the Western powers would intervene. They had seen the strength of the West. If Japan went to war her reform projects would be held up and she would be vulnerable to an onslaught by Russia from Sakhalin.

Saigō was furious. Like Achilles sulking in his tent, he withdrew from the government whose chief military leader he had been, and returned to the Satsuma domain in Kyūshū, where he began to train young *samurai* in the arts of war. His warriors were on the march in 1877, with the support of almost the whole island of Kyūshū. But the government garrison of Kumamoto held out against him, and Japan's new conscript army—peasants officered by *samurai*—under a Chōshū *samurai*, Yamagata, defeated Saigō's 30,000 men. Rather than fall into the hands of his opponents, Saigō had himself killed by one of his lieutenants.

Two things were clear from Saigō's defeat: armed rebellion against the central government did not pay, even when it was led by the most popular of Japan's military heroes. And even the age-old *samurai* virtues were no match for the numbers and weapons of the new national conscript army.

Left: *Japan's embassy, headed by Prince Iwakura, leaves Yokohama for the USA and Europe.* **Next page:** *Last stand of the old-style* samurai—*Saigō and warriors in the 1877 revolt*

原國幹

西郷隆盛

桐野利秋

Chapter 1
The Meiji Restoration and Political Change

The course of government was uncertain in the first days of the Meiji Restoration. At first an attempt was made to recreate a medieval 'Grand Council of State' *(Dajōkan)* supervising a number of departments. One office, that of Shintō Worship *(Jingikan)*, outranked even the Grand Council of State itself, since Buddhism was to be disestablished and state Shintō (see Chapter 2) encouraged to reinforce the newly recovered Imperial system. In 1885 a system of cabinet government was introduced on the Prussian model, and in 1889 the Emperor granted his people a new constitution. This set up a National Assembly, or Diet, consisting of a House of Peers and an elected House of Representatives, the first elections for which were held in 1890.

The tightly controlled separation of the classes of society under the *bakufu* (nobility and clergy, soldiers, peasants and artisans, merchants, outcasts) was modified and ultimately dissolved. Firstly the court nobles and the feudal lords *(daimyō)* were linked together as peers. Then the *samurai* became gentry *(shizoku)* but gradually lost their special privileges. The rest were included in the general category of *heimin* (commoner) and, by a decree of 1870, were permitted to have family names as well as personal names. In 1871 the wearing of swords and the cutting of hair in *samurai* style were made optional instead of compulsory, and the *samurai*'s right to cut down a commoner *(kirisute-gomen)* for a supposed or real insult was withdrawn. Sword-wearing was finally forbidden in 1876. Farmers were allowed to ride on horseback along the public highway in 1871, and in the same year regulations limiting types of clothing to be worn by commoners were withdrawn. Social outcasts, the *eta* who dealt in leather and skins and were therefore shunned as pariahs, and *hinin* (beggars), were drawn into the commoner class and, in theory at any rate, the notion of social outcast was abolished.

Left: On 6th April 1868 the Emperor Meiji issued the Five Articles of the Imperial Covenant, setting out the fundamentals of national policy. Here he listens while the Covenant is read

Political opposition was active. Since there was no formal institutionalised opposition, and the crushing of Saigō's rebellion had shown the futility of armed resistance, a number of political parties were formed, led by *samurai* from fiefs like Hizen and Tosa who felt that the two major clans, Satsuma and Chōshū, were monopolising power. They were right. Well into the 20th century, with one or two brief exceptions, Japanese government was carried on by an alternation of prime ministers appointed from one or other of these two clans. The feudal lords, or *daimyō*, had given in to the request of their younger *samurai* to put the good of the nation before the retention of their feudal domains, and signed over their lands and powers to the Emperor. This was not entirely disinterested. They received large blocks of shares in government enterprises in exchange for their previous rice-tributes, and their deprivation of status was compensated for by the creation of a new peerage in 1884 which made them princes, marquises, counts, viscounts, or barons in the new Meiji nobility.

The birth of the political parties

Conspicuous by their absence from the first honours lists were two men who had been part of the early Meiji government: Itagaki Taisuke, of Tosa, and Ōkuma Shigenobu, of Hizen. Both of them were resolutely nationalist. But instead of combining this with an old-fashioned conservatism as the court noble Iwakura did, or a new authoritarian conservatism like that of the Chōshū *samurai* Itō, these two protested against the usurpation of Imperial power by what was (in their view) a system of arbitrary decisions imposed by a few individuals acting in the Emperor's name. 'The people whose duty it is to pay taxes to the government,' declared Itagaki in a petition of 1874, 'have the right to share in the government's affairs and to approve or condemn.' Itagaki had been influenced by the writings of the French Enlightenment, and the Liberal Party *(Jiyūtō)* which he founded in 1881 was aimed at securing constitutional government, the extension of popular rights *(minken)*, and Japan's achievement of equality with other nations.

In the same year Okuma Shigenobu, like Itagaki temporarily in the political wilderness as the result of a quarrel with Itō, founded the Reform Party *(Kaishintō)* which was less radical and looked for support to the wealthy middle classes and the Westernised intelligentsia who saw the British parliamentary system as the

Left: The Emperor and his entourage enter in splendour Tokyo castle, the new imperial residence, on 28th November 1868

ideal at which Japan should aim. Once the House of Representatives became a part of Japanese political life, in 1890, Ōkuma fought long and hard to give the parties a responsible role and to make the cabinet take notice of them. It was not easy. Cabinets were formed as a rule without any reference to the strength of parties in the Diet, and the new parties were subject to constant harassment by the police.

Japan's new constitution was promulgated in 1889. It was the work of Itō Hirobumi and his advisers, and was consciously based on the Prussian model, since Itō had remained a fervent admirer of Bismarck. Itō was careful to insist that the constitution had not been 'won' by the people, but was the Emperor's gift, and the Emperor's power was safeguarded in the initial clauses. A legislature was set up, with two houses: the Upper House was based on the new peerage, the Lower House was to be elected, but their powers were limited. Decisions on whether laws were constitutional or not were made not by the Supreme Court but by the Privy Council, of which Itō himself was President, as he intended to keep the reins of government firmly in his own hands. A revision of cabinet regulations in December 1889 provided that the War Minister and the Navy Minister should be almost independent of their civilian colleagues and have direct access to the Throne, a decision which was to have far-reaching effects in the next half-century. The electoral basis was small: out of Japan's 40,000,000 population, only one in eighty was entitled to vote.

Military demands

Factionalism and corruption soon played havoc with the political parties, and, in spite of the civic courage of some of their leaders, they soon caved in to military pressure during the 1894-5 war with China, and meekly voted military appropriations even when the 1894 budget was twice as large as that for 1890. Military control over the cabinet was exercised by the Chōshū *samurai,* Yamagata, later Field Marshal and several times Prime Minister. Where Itō had provided a strong, centralising, Emperor-focused, governmental structure, where Itagaki and Ōkuma had given to the opposition the liberal ideals of Western enlightenment, Yamagata bequeathed to modern

*Far right: Diagram of the 1889 Prussian-style constitution, showing the ominous lack of accountability on the part of the armed services (**top**); the Emperor, opening the first session of the Diet, hands the imperial edict to the Prime Minister, Itō Hirobumi (**bottom**). Right: The giants of the Meiji era – (left-hand column from top) the Emperor Meiji, Itō Hirobumi, Ōkubo Toshimichi, Prince Iwakura, (right-hand column) Yamagata Aritomo, Ōkuma Shigenobu, Inoue Kaoru, Saionji Kimmochi*

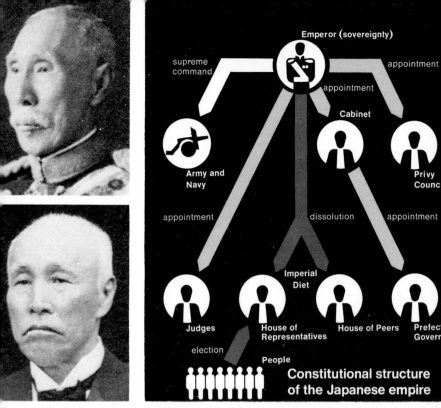

Constitutional structure of the Japanese empire

Emperor (sovereignty)

supreme command

appointment

appointment

Cabinet

Army and Navy

Privy Council

appointment

dissolution

appointment

Imperial Diet

Judges

House of Representatives

House of Peers

Prefectural Governors

election

People

Japan its Pandora's Box: a powerful national army. When his colleagues had gone off to Europe and America to study constitutions, Yamagata toured the armies of the West. The introduction of conscription in 1872 and the defeat of Saigō's romantic last stand in 1877 were his work. Yamagata was far from being a simple Colonel Blimp. It is true that party rivalry symbolised for him the usurpation of true constitutionalism by selfish passions; but he believed strongly in local government as the foundation of the state, and, although he encompassed China's defeat in 1894, he had no wish to destroy the Chinese Imperial system. Like many Japanese, he would have preferred a strong China able to defend itself against Western depredations, and to which Japan could ally herself in the common task of defending Asia. He was sure the world was going to face a violent clash between the white and non-white races, and Japan and China should be, in his view, the leaders of the non-white world. He aimed to secure the independence of the Army and Navy Ministers from partisan politics and ensured, by a decree passed in 1895, that no civilian could hold either portfolio.

When Itō saw how much Yamagata's influence and prestige had grown since the victory in the Sino-Japanese War, he decided that he needed civilian support just as Yamagata had achieved strong military backing, and from a disparate grouping of landlord interests and old Liberal Party members, Itō founded the 'Political Friends Association' *(Seiyūkai)* in 1900 as his own party, though he had little belief in the value of party politics. The Meiji cabinets and parties give a very strong impression of being a game of 'musical chairs' played in deadly seriousness. Apart from Ōkuma Shigenobu, who seems to have been less prepared to compound, men with apparently irreconcilable views suddenly accepted cabinet posts which implied interdependence, because objectives could be achieved not through parties but through personalities.

Left: Japan prepares to enter the world stage by becoming a power in her own right. Top: Infantrymen in the new conscript army. Bottom: British-trained sailors on board a training ship

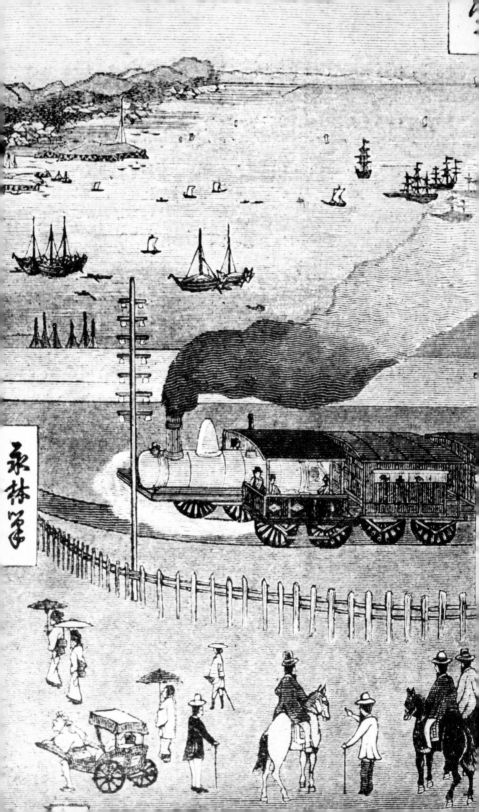

Chapter 2
Japan Modernises

Foreign oppression and political upheavals are not the whole story of any people. There is a more intimate side, harder to know, but perhaps more revealing of that people's true nature: the way they worship their gods, the food they eat, the clothes they wear, and how they travel from place to place. In these things too, as well as in public policy, the men of Meiji carried out a revolution in Japanese life.

RELIGION AND EDUCATION

Under the Tokugawa shogunate, Buddhism was incorporated into the state system: all households were required to register with a local Buddhist temple, and this provided a convenient census as well as a means of keeping a watchful eye on the people through the temple reports. One of the first achievements of the men of the Meiji Restoration in their attempts to create a centralised, authoritarian, monarchical state was to replace Buddhism in this function by Shintō. An early law of Meiji — withdrawn later because of its unpopularity — insisted on everyone enrolling in the Shintō shrine nearest his home. Not only this, but the easy-going mutual coexistence of Buddhism and Shintō was brought to an end by the government's Separation Edict, the purpose of which was to stress Shintō as the really indigenous way of life for a Japanese, one more closely linked with the Imperial system. So the Department of Shintō Affairs was set up and given a status outranking even that of the Grand Council of State.

Shintō is basically a deification of natural phenomena and the ancestors of the people, and means literally 'the way of the gods'. The gods in question, who are not held to be omnipotent or omniscient, are called *kami* by the Japanese, and are really tutelary deities of a given neighbourhood or cult. The rites attached to them are employed at certain crucial moments in the individual's life — the threshold of manhood, marriage, the funeral ceremony.

Left: *The opening ceremony in Tokyo of the first railway line in Japan, 1872. Few thought it important enough to attend*

23

Now, traditionally, the Japanese funeral ceremony was Buddhist, but from early Meiji onwards attempts were made to substitute Shintō funeral rites. In 1871 the Department of Shintō Affairs became a ministry, and was given the task of educating the Japanese people in loyalty to the Imperial throne, obedience to authority, and reverence for the *kami*. Not only Shintō priests, but Buddhist priests, Confucian scholars, and even professional fortune-tellers were induced to take part in this programme: by 1874 there were reputed to be 7,000 of them active in Japan, in spite of the fact that compulsory Shintō registration was withdrawn in 1873. Buddhism, as one more link with the feudalism of the Tokugawa, had to be disestablished, and those Buddhist priests who had connections with Shintō shrines had to become Shintō priests or leave the shrines. In 1871 the even more startling measure of confiscating temple lands was carried out, and the Imperial household put an end to Buddhist ceremonies in the Palace. In one place, Toyama, hundreds of Buddhist temples were reduced to seven overnight. To some extent, these measures were undertaken because Buddhist prohibitions stood in the way of Westernisation. Westerners ate meat, so the prohibition against that had to go. So did begging and the prohibition of marriage for Buddhist priests.

To emphasise the Emperor cult, Shintō shrines were erected to the ancestors of the Imperial clan inside the Palace, as a substitute for the Buddhist memorial services. In addition, a shrine was built in Tokyo for those who had died on behalf of the Imperial cause during the disturbances of the Restoration. This shrine, later known as the Yasukuni Shrine, was to become the focus of militarist devotion to the Emperor in years to come. The custom of celebrating the Emperor's birthday as a national holiday was introduced, and the Emperor himself was considered as having become a *kami* in his lifetime, which was a deliberate harking-back to the titles of the earliest Japanese Emperors ('living *kami*, ruler of the world below, emperor of the realm of Yamato').

The use of Shintō to bolster up the Imperial restoration laid the foundations for a paradoxical state of affairs. The system was also strengthened by the adoption of whatever was thought most useful in Western society, and those who made contact with the West were drawn to ideas which made turning back to the past — inherent in the reinvigoration of Shintō — quite purposeless. For some, the answer lay in Christianity, and the return of

Right: Shintō was used to bolster the state system. Top: Court officials about to take part in a Shintō festival. Bottom: A Tokyo booth selling wooden shrines for the household god shelf

Europeans to Japan had uncovered tiny communities of Christian survivors in the southern island of Kyūshū, who had kept their faith through centuries of persecution and lack of priests. For others, the rationalism of Europe was more attractive, since it offered, as Shintō did not, the prize of *bummei kaika* – 'enlightenment and civilisation' – the catchwords of the Meiji Era.

Western *versus* Confucian ideals

In other words, Japan had an educational problem. In the Tokugawa schools, elementary skills had been taught along with conventional Confucian morality, centred round filial piety and respect for the powers-that-be (in practice, at any rate). This kind of Confucianism could have played a similar role under Meiji, but it had competitors not only among the 'scholars of Japanese learning' *(kokugaku-sha),* i.e. the Shintō revivalists, but also among the apostles of Western education *(yōgaku-sha).* One of these left his ideas and personality firmly imprinted on Japan: the former *samurai* Fukuzawa Yūkichi. Fukuzawa, who had lived in America and Europe, founded a private school (later the Keiō University) and a newspaper to spread Westernisation, and he put the blame for Japan's temporary backwardness on her study of Chinese philosophy. 'In the education of the East,' he wrote, 'saturated with Confucian principles, I find two things missing: studies in number and reason in material culture, and the notion of independence in spiritual culture. Japan cannot assert her position among the world's great nations unless she acknowledges these principles.'

Fukuzawa was described by an English contemporary as 'the intellectual father of half the young men who now fill the middle and lower posts in the government of Japan' and as leading Young Japan 'in ostentatiously denying the importance of all religious dogmas'. It was owing to the initiative of supporters of Western ideas that the government brought in a system of universal education in 1872, based partly on the French system. This was soon in the hands of men who believed the Confucian classics should be brought back into the schoolroom and moral teaching made the most important subject in the primary curriculum. A succession of Education Ordinances in the mid-1880s asserted the supremacy of the state at every level from primary school to university, and in 1890 the Imperial Rescript on Education was issued, stressing service to the state, not the individual's self-betterment, as the educational ideal:

'These form the fundamental principles of education for Our subjects [*it ran*]: be filial to your relations, as hus-

Right: Geishas—traditionally trained as models of behaviour

26

bands and wives, and faithful to your friends; let your conduct be courteous and frugal, and love others as yourself; attend to your studies and practise your respective callings; cultivate your intellectual faculties and train your moral feelings; foster the public weal and promote the interests of society; always give strict obedience to the Constitution and all the laws of Our Empire, display your public spirit and courage, and thereby give Us your support in promoting and maintaining the honour and prosperity of Our Empire, which is coeval with the heavens and the earth.'

The government had laudable plans for ensuring the education of every child, but it soon ran out of funds, and children had to be paid for by their parents at the rate of 50 *sen* a month. This may not seem much by modern standards, but in the 1870s it was the equivalent of a quarter of a bushel of rice, and was a big outlay for a poor family. By the end of Meiji in 1912, in spite of claims of 95 per cent school attendance, literacy was by no means nation-wide.

A survey of twenty-two factories in 1892 showed that out of 5,680 workers close on one-third were still of school age and well over half of them had received no education at all. In a factory of 800 workers surveyed in 1918, over 400 women and 95 men had not completed primary education, though a four-year compulsory period had been introduced in 1886.

The universities began under similar drawbacks. When Tokyo University received *samurai* students from the feudal domains in 1870, they all wore swords to lectures and were compelled to use interpreters to listen to their English or German lecturers, most of whom knew no Japanese. Many were rich enough to keep themselves, but some were very poor, and later in the century it was not unknown for students to work their way through university as clerks or even as rickshaw pullers.

The Ministry of Education kept a firm centralising control over the schools by vetting the textbooks used, and, like the conscript peasant army of the new Japan, the system had a unifying effect. It created citizens apt in the elementary skills of primary schooling and imbued with general Confucian principles of loyalty to the State and its institutions, focused upon the Emperor as the keystone of the entire national structure. It was not meant to produce questioning minds. The very apex of the system, Tokyo Imperial University (so renamed in 1886), became in effect an institution for the training of Japan's higher

*Top left: A street scene in Odawara, 1879—heavy wooden wheels and man-drawn carts still lingered on. **Bottom:** Many samurai became businessmen, these found it harder to adapt*

bureaucracy. The staff of the university was under government control, and the President was directly responsible to the Minister of Education and through him to the Emperor. The professors had to take oaths to the government, and the purpose of their teaching was defined in the act of establishment as 'to teach and investigate those mysteries of science and learning, of arts and crafts, which are of practical service to the needs of the State'.

FOOD

Asked what the staple Japanese food was, most people would answer 'rice'. In fact the story is much more complex. The Tax Revision Bureau of the Ministry of Finance reported in 1874 that, in the provinces at any rate, only one-third of the amount spent on food was spent on rice. The contrast is between town and country. The countryman produced the rice, but by and large, as under the *bakufu,* he was too poor to eat it regularly. Even in the cities some people could only afford the coarser grains, wheat and barley, mixed with a few vegetables. During the Meiji era the importation of foreign rice began to alter this picture, as did the introduction of meat.

The unit of measurement of rice was the *koku,* roughly equal to 5 bushels. An official survey in 1877 showed that in the towns and cities the average annual rice consumption per person was $1\frac{1}{4}$ *koku,* say 6 bushels a year. In the countryside, it was nearly half a *koku* less per person. The reason for this was relatively simple: under the *bakufu,* 55 per cent of the total rice crop had to be handed over to the local lord, who usually retained about one-third; the rest went to the big cities and castle towns to feed the *samurai* and the townspeople. In 1873 payment of tax in rice ceased, and a land tax of 3% took its place. But the small farmer was no better off. Changes in the diet took place first in the cities, and then – with improved transportation – in the outlying country areas.

On the whole, rice consumption was regulated by local rather than national conditions. In feudal times each feudal district tried to be self-supporting, as indeed each farmer did, and there was no question of exporting rice to other districts in time of shortage. One of the Tokugawa shogunate's control measures was to enforce prohibitions on travel between fiefs, which inhibited exchange of goods between them. So an individual fief could be very hard hit when famine struck. The fief of Tsugaru lost about 600,000 bushels of rice in the year 1782, and two years later 81,700 people had died of famine. The north of Japan suffered particularly hard. When the fief barriers disappeared with the Meiji Restoration some equalisation of food conditions became possible, but it was the foreign crops which made the big difference.

There might have been famine on the 18th-century scale in 1869 when the rice crop dropped to 37·5 per cent of the annual average. That year, 648,285 *koku* of foreign rice were brought into Japan, and the much larger figure of 2,150,843 *koku* the following year. Japan profited from the rich crop of French Indo-China, the source of most of this imported rice. Later the Japanese began to export rice themselves. Over 750,000 *koku* were exported in 1878 owing to famine in China, and again in 1891 when the value of rice exported rose to more than 3,500,000 *yen*.

The availability of foreign rice did not make its mark at once. Even poor people would not eat rice from China or Korea, claiming that its flavour was inferior to that of the home product. Merchants then hit upon the device of mixing it with Japanese rice in the proportion of 3:7 but this was later prohibited. The average consumption of rice in Japan increased from 3½ bushels per person per year in 1868 to over 5 bushels in the decade before 1914. Better methods of cultivation increased national production: the average harvest went up from nearly 30,000,000 *koku* in the period from 1878 to 1882 to over 50,000,000 *koku* in the period from 1908 to 1912, though the area under cultivation only increased by one-sixth.

The introduction of meat

Whatever the reason (Buddhist prejudice against taking life, for instance), the Japanese were not meat-eaters on any significant scale under the Tokugawa. Though game (boar and deer) was eaten, it was felt to be unclean to eat the flesh of horses and cattle, and, as late as 1869, of a group of people on Hachijojima who had killed and eaten an ox, ten were banished, ten lost their jobs, and three others received public reprimands. There is an interesting passage in the biography of the socialist revolutionary Katayama Sen which shows that the Japanese feeling for their domestic animals made killing them repugnant: 'I was born in a farmhouse and worked as a farmer. The family ox was absolutely necessary for the ploughing, and we loved him as if he were one of the family. I used to follow him in the fields, and it was from his labour that I earned money. I had so many memories of him that I would never have wanted to eat meat.'

But urban populations had no such diffidence, and the presence of foreign meat-eating communities in such places as Yokohama soon spread the habit. Meat, which had been referred to metaphorically as 'mountain whale' *('yama kujira'),* was soon spoken of directly and great virtues were claimed for it. A butcher's shop in Tokyo advertised in 1867: 'Meat is good for you. It gives you

Left: Peasants on the terraced slopes of a tea plantation

31

energy, strength, and vitality if you are well or sick . . . Choice meats are sold here as cheaply as possible. We will show you the best cuts and the tastiest morsels; which to use for roasting, which for boiling, which for stewing.'

Methods of cooking were not European but Japanese, and the dish *sukiyaki*, thin strips of meat boiled with vegetables and bean curd, became popular. The poor could indulge, since thin strips could be bought ready-cooked on skewers. Because meat was shunned at first, it was served in low-down eating houses. Fukuzawa Yūkichi describes how he used to visit two such places in Ōsaka when he was a student: 'The clientele consisted of liberally tattooed ruffians and students. No one cared where the meat came from, or whether the cow had been slaughtered or had died of disease. For fifteen *cash* they served you a plentiful helping of beef, *sake* [rice wine], and rice, but the meat was tough and smelly.'

Officialdom backed the butchers in their desire to encourage meat-eating. 'Meat is a nourishing food that helps people keep in good spirits and strengthens the blood,' read a proclamation from the Tsuruga Prefectural Office in 1872. 'But some people, bound by conservative habits, not only refuse to eat it themselves but declare it to be unclean and say that those who eat it cannot appear before the gods. This is nothing but bigotry. If there are any such people in the neighbourhood, the town officials should visit them and explain the value of meat to them.'

There was other meat besides beef. Pork had been known in southern Kyūshū (being nearest to China), and horsemeat was a cheaper alternative to beef. One Japanese remembered his schooldays in the 1890s when the boys would buy horsemeat. Real beef cost 30 to 40 *sen* a lb., whereas for 10 *sen* they could get 7 or 8 lbs. of horsemeat 'so fresh that the blood was still running out'.

Foreign appetites also required vegetables different from those Japan provided, and it was not long before market gardens grew strange plants such as cabbage, asparagus, onions, cauliflower, and tomato. On the other hand, Japanese cooking did not suit these vegetables, and acceptance of them as part of the native diet was slow. Other elements of foreign diet came in rapidly in the late 19th century: dairy products such as milk, butter, and cheese; white sugar (which was very valuable and sold in pharmacies as medicine); and tinned foods (particularly sardines and whale meat), which were introduced in the 1870s. The Sino-Japanese War proved to be the canning industries' great opportunity, when Japan's armies needed supplies of tinned meat.

Right: Amidst the hurry to modernise, the old-style courtesies continued: a group of people drinking sake *and smoking*

Population growth, 1700–1950

figures in thousands

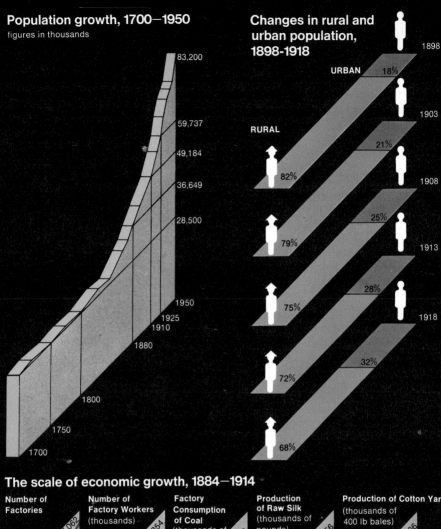

83,200

59,737

49,184

36,649

28,500

1950
1925
1910

1880

1800

1750

1700

Changes in rural and urban population, 1898-1918

1898

URBAN   18%

RURAL

1903

82%   21%

1908

79%   25%

1913

75%   28%

1918

72%   32%

68%

The scale of economic growth, 1884–1914

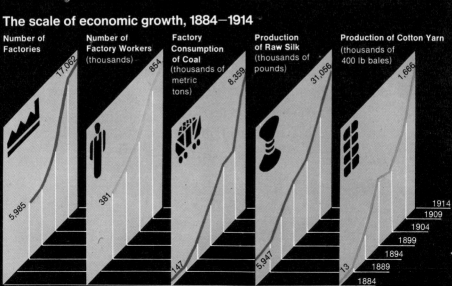

Number of Factories

17,062

5,985

Number of Factory Workers (thousands)

854

381

Factory Consumption of Coal (thousands of metric tons)

8,359

147

Production of Raw Silk (thousands of pounds)

31,056

5,947

Production of Cotton Yarn (thousands of 400 lb bales)

1,666

13

1914
1909
1904
1899
1894
1889
1884

It was the army, in fact, which experimented with Western food. The meal at home was still essentially Japanese-style, and it was rare for a Japanese family to sit round a table on chairs and eat with knives and forks. The lunch-box *(bentō-bako)* made of wood at first, and later of aluminium, was popular and usually contained half a dozen balls of rice, wrapped in seaweed flakes *(nori)* with some pickles and a piece of fish. The army offered a young man more than this, with the chance to drink beer and eat beef. It is interesting to see that four years after the Russo-Japanese War a home for disabled veterans was serving weekly, besides plentiful rice and vegetables, beef three times, pork once, egg eight times, and fish eight times. The soldier's diet was superior to the civilian's, and often the army would be the first user of bread and tinned meat in any district. By the end of the Meiji era Japan's diet was, with the exception of those of Malaya and Manchuria, the best in the Far East, though it was short on protein, minerals, and vitamins, largely because rice had become the dominant element.

CLOTHING

The wealthier Japanese always had a great variety of beautiful textiles with which to adorn themselves—silks, satins, and elaborate brocades; but most of the people were clothed in cotton or hemp, not simply because they could afford no better but because the *bakufu* government issued strict orders on types of clothing to be worn, in order to keep the social classes visibly apart. So an ordinance of 1643 limited local lords to silk pongee, hemp, and cotton, and ordinary farmers to hemp and cotton only. 'A merchant wearing fine silks is an ugly sight,' wrote the novelist Saikaku in 1688. 'Homespun is not only more suited to his station, but he looks smarter in it.' Whether or not Saikaku had his tongue in his cheek when he praised the Clothing Edicts which were issued on many occasions during the Tokugawa shogunate, his own stories are proof that many people in the cities dressed as richly as they pleased, whatever their official status.

'Of recent years,' he writes, 'ever since some ingenious Kyoto creatures started the fashion, every variety of splendid material has been used for men's and women's clothes, and the drapers' sample-books have blossomed in a riot of colour. What with delicate Ukiyo stencil-patterns, multi-coloured "Imperial" designs, and dappled motifs in wash-graded tints . . . every device on earth has been exhausted . . . garments of three distinct layers—scarlet crêpe enclosed within translucent walls of delicate white silk—and garments with sleeves and neck-pieces stiffened

Left: Diagrams showing Japan's rapid industrialisation, pre-1914

466,126

1907
1911

553,390

with padding. Such things were unheard of in former times.'

But Saikaku is describing the townsman. In the country, where life was harsh and it was difficult to get enough to eat, the edicts can have caused little disturbance of mind or vanity. The changes brought about by the opening of the country to foreign trade resulted in the edicts on clothing being abolished and in the availability of cheap cotton goods. As far as poor people were concerned, hemp production was still vital and statistics show that it increased until the mid-1890s. Even when other textiles began to be used for clothing it was still needed for fishing nets and ropes. But by the 1890s, largely because it took from four to eight times as much labour to weave cloth from hemp as it did from cotton, hemp fell into disuse.

The Japanese have never relied on animal fibre for clothing, but besides hemp and cotton there were a number of vegetable fibres with versatile uses: wisteria, sedge, rushes, and reeds have all been pressed into service, and rice straw has been used for footwear. Manufactured materials replaced all these during the Meiji period. The army heralded changes in fashion. Modern European-style uniforms were more suitable to modern weapons and accoutrements than the older *samurai* garments, however picturesque. And wool, introduced from Europe in the 16th century, was not in common use until it was employed for military uniforms. It must be remembered that the old *samurai* clothing was not a 'utility garment' —it had ceremonial functions and the wearer's dignity, rather than his efficiency as a fighting man, was involved. Since the status of the *samurai* was among the first things to be hit by the new reforms, his upkeep of ceremonial clothing became pointless, which must have been a great relief to the poorer members of the class. By the late 1860s a number of nobles at the Imperial Court in Kyoto had begun to appear in Western costume, and in November 1867 the use of Western clothing was authorised throughout the army and navy. Rather sadly the two houses of Yamashina and Takakura, which had long supplied the Imperial wardrobe, were dismissed in August 1871, and in November 1872 the Court ordered Western dress to be used for all formal occasions, at least for men.

Women retained the old ceremonial costume longer, but by the middle of the 1880s Japanese society ladies were wearing Western dresses to balls and dances. The new style received prompt Imperial approval:

'The modern Western outfit for women consists of an upper and lower garment and is therefore in accordance

Right: *Western dress replaced traditional Japanese wear for formal occasions; ministers leave after an Imperial audience*

with the ancient Japanese system of dress,' the Empress wrote. 'Furthermore, it is suitable for ceremonial use and is convenient in that it allows freedom of movement. It is therefore most proper that the Western method of sewing be imitated.'

Uniforms were not confined to the army and navy. Always very sensitive to rank and position, the Japanese had various uniforms for schoolboys, nurses, mill-workers, railwaymen, and postmen. Schoolgirls wore the traditional *hakama* trimmed with the school colours at first, and were among the last to adopt Western styles.

Traditional customs go west

Hair became a problem. It was not an unfamiliar sight to see a well-to-do Japanese-about-town in the 1870s, having shed his Japanese costume and wearing a Euro-pean morning coat, with his hair still unruly and un-kempt from shaving off his topknot. In some schools in Tokyo in the 1880s boys and girls still wore *kimono,* and the boys kept the traditional *coiffure* which demanded special preparation each morning before they set out. But hair-styles too were soon vulnerable to the European in-vasion. One particular restaurant-cum-ballroom in Tokyo, the famous *Rokumeikan* (Pavilion of the Deer Call), was the centre of fashion from its establishment in 1883, and Japanese ladies showed off their latest dresses and hair-styles on lavish occasions there.

As with the more complex foreign foods, the sartorial problems and heartaches of the capital found little echo in the farms of rural Japan, where the peasant went about his task in loin-cloth or trousers. The sheer functionalism of this clothing made it not dissimilar to Western work-clothes, so when these became cheaply available there was no difficulty in passing from one to the other.

Underwear was a different matter. Vests and under-pants of muslin and flannel made their appearance in the cities by 1873. In the country men continued to wear the loin-cloth. This garment had been seen quite commonly on the streets in the period immediately before the Meiji Restoration. Nakedness was not prohibited by law until 1871, when the Tokyo government regulated against it:

'The common people of this city, instead of wearing clothes, go out to work or to the bath virtually naked. This is a general custom and Japanese are not inclined to criticise it; but in foreign countries it is looked down upon. Westerners consider it shameful to reveal their bodies, and they do not do it. Recently we have come into much closer contact with other countries, and many foreigners have come to Japan. If this ugly practice is left as it is, it will bring shame on our nation. Henceforward no one, not even the poorest, shall go naked.'

Western mores insisted on other changes in Japanese life. A series of articles pretending to be a Western observer's views of Japan appeared in the *Jiji Shimpō* in 1900:

'The next astonishing thing is the fact that Japanese women urinate on the streets. With the exception of Tokyo and the Kantō area, this practice persists in all parts of the country, including Kyoto and Ōsaka. Although the sight is too revolting to describe, even Japanese ladies of the middle class or better consider it no shame whatever, and one is likely to see a gentleman in fine clothing doing something quite distressing at a busy intersection.'

A fashion free-for-all

Some of the clothing changes were sudden, hectic, and ill-considered. Men were often unsure what went with what, and it was not unusual to find a man retaining *kimono* but wearing European boots or shoes with it. The country postman would wear straw sandals with his new-style uniform, and the schoolboy would tie his trousers with an *obi*. The sheer ugliness of the mixture was one factor which induced a greater simplicity of approach in the 1890s and, with the victory in the Russo-Japanese War and the country's increasing self-confidence, a return to native styles.

The army led in the introduction of European headgear in 1871 and within two decades every Western style of hat was introduced, straw cadies, panamas, hunting hats — photographs of authors in *kimono* but topped by battered trilbies are by no means uncommon frontispieces to literary biographies. Shoes came in with military uniforms and were worn as alternatives to *geta* (wooden clogs), *tabi* (cotton socks with the big toe separated from the rest, often with a thick sole) or, in the country, *zōri* (straw sandals). In the cities a determined effort was made to ensure that people did not go barefoot, and a Tokyo police ordinance of May 1901 forbade anyone to walk around barefoot 'as a precaution against the plague'. For everyday purposes shoes were not as convenient as Japanese footwear, since the Japanese remove them on entering a house.

Cosmetics, which had played an important part in Japanese life from early times, underwent similar changes. 'Until her dying day,' wrote the daughter of a woman of the *samurai* class, 'my mother never appeared without liprouge and thick powder.' Women's hair was often so carefully arranged it looked like a wig, and this was typical of the formal, stiff, and uncomfortable style of the late Tokugawa period. Men were as careful, and pulled

Left: Anglo-Japanese friendship at a Tokyo garden-party, 1905

their topknots tight in the style called *Honda-mage* (or *chon'mage*); nearly all the hair on the top of the head was shaved off, the hair brought together and tied at the back, and the pigtail thus formed was stiffened with heavy pomade and brought forward over the smoothly shaved crown. This meant shaving the crown of the head about twice a week, and can hardly have been a popular style. Yet its abolition, in favour of Western hair-styles, was resisted with physical violence in Kumamoto and had to be reinforced by a 50-*sen* fine on topknots in Wakamatsu.

Then there was the shaving of eyebrows and their replacement by artificial ones, and the blackening of teeth. 'What could be more tasteless than for women to blacken their teeth and shave their eyebrows?' queried a magazine in 1875. 'By doing so they lose their natural beauty and make themselves appear deformed. If such evil customs are not prohibited by law, the opportunities for a new age will be lost.'

The magazine was two years behind the Imperial Court. On 3rd March 1873, the Empress had appeared in public wearing her own eyebrows and with unblackened teeth. Tokyo rapidly followed suit, though the provinces did not catch on for some time.

The frenetic introduction of Western styles ultimately gave way to a double standard for clothing, hats, and footwear. Western costume was appropriate to modern urban and industrial life, and was worn in offices or factories and in the services. In the home the traditional costume was more suitable – it was not, for one thing, easy to kneel or sit on *tatami* while wearing trousers. On the whole women's fashions changed less abruptly than men's. Women were more confined to the home, and the house itself imposed its own appropriateness.

TRANSPORT AND TRAVEL

'In China,' says Somerset Maugham in a celebrated passage, 'it is man who is the beast of burden.' The same was true of Tokugawa Japan. Oxen pulled the plough, but on the roads of Japan goods were carried by men, as were the palanquins of the feudal lords. Horses were sometimes used. The roads were narrow and unmetalled, crossed difficult terrain – rivers and mountain barriers – and were interrupted by check-points where a travelling *daimyō*'s retinue might be searched for *de-onna iri-deppō* – 'women going out, guns going in'. The rice tribute was taken to the big cities by boat. All this changed with the introduction of the metal wheel.

Top left: *The interior and exterior of Japan's first spinning factory to apply mass-production techniques, opened in 1872.*
Bottom: *A Tokyo street in 1874. In the centre is the Mitsui Bank*

The primitive carts which were available in Edo and Ōsaka were clumsy and heavy wooden-wheeled vehicles. The metal wheel made it possible to have lighter transport—also man-drawn—of a kind which has been for so long associated with the East in the European mind that it seems to have existed forever: the rickshaw. Yet the rickshaw is a very recent invention. 'The form was very simple,' runs an early description. 'Around a seat platform with curtains hanging on all four sides four columns were erected, and a top was placed thereon. This was set on wheels. The whole thing was made of plain wood. At first there was no hood, and when it rained oil paper was used for a covering.' The first rickshaw factory seems to have been set up in 1869 and two years later there were reputed to be 25,000 rickshaws in Tokyo. The figure may be exaggerated, but soon rickshaws were being exported to China and the South Seas and by 1882 had reached Hong Kong and Singapore. The rickshaws began to acquire improvements: some were heated by charcoal heaters in winter, others had newspapers for their riders to read on the journey, and a final luxurious development came with rubber tyres in 1903. The rickshawmen were not as keen on these as the riders were. 'We asked two pullers whether the rubber tyres made their work easier or not,' wrote a reporter in the *Niroku Newspaper* on 12th September 1909. 'One said they were light and easy to pull, but the other said that while they were light enough they tired him because they did not make any noise. The clanging of the old iron wheels, he explained, stirred up his spirit of competition and made him feel like working.'

The rickshaw soon began to create its own hierarchy. Gangs of pullers would be hired by a boss who gave them a small cut on the charge. Some of this they would have to pay out in the hilly parts of Tokyo to the lowest of the low, gangs of extra pullers or pushers who helped them up the steeper slopes. It was quite common in the early days for down-and-out *samurai* to act as rickshaw pullers and they competed with out-of-work palanquin bearers for jobs. Some had the reputation of being able to cover 50 to 60 miles a day. Sharp practices naturally arose—taking travellers the long way round, asking more than the agreed fare, so that the police stepped in and began to regulate not merely fares but behaviour and costume. In Tokyo rickshaw men had to be at least eighteen years old, know the city well, and wear hats, trousers, and working coats, blue in winter and white in summer. They formed themselves into unions, and rival unions—often no more

Top right: *Rickshawman.* **Bottom:** *Victorian Japan—a station and trains on the first railway line between Tokyo and Yokohama*

than gangs – fought for favoured spots outside the railway stations. There were also the aristocrats, or Jeeveses, of the rickshaw world, who would work for only one client, were paid monthly, and were fed and lodged in their client's home. By the end of the century there were about 50,000 in Tokyo alone.

Most rickshaws were for one passenger, but a double rickshaw was introduced and promptly banned by some local authorities as conducive to immorality. One newspaper reported in 1875: 'Now the men who show off by rubbing knees and making love with prostitutes, as well as the ones who make overtures to respectable young women riding with them, have had their hopes dashed. Ugly practices have been swept away in one happy moment.'

First the horse-drawn bus, then the tram, sounded the death-knell of the rickshaw. A tram service was opened in Tokyo in 1903, and by the following year many rickshaw men were not making enough to live on. Those rickshaws which ran a relay service along the highroads were put out of business by the trains, but some compensation was found in outlying areas by pullers working from railway stations.

It seems likely that the idea of the rickshaw originated with the sight of the horse and carriage, the equipage of the wealthy foreigner. It was the foreigner too who brought in the railway. The first line, 18 miles long, was built between Tokyo and Yokohama in 1872, and a line linking Ōsaka with Kyoto followed four years later. Soon the whole country was covered with a network of railways, and by 1911 there were 5,506 miles of them. By the mid-1870s, 1,750,000 passengers a year travelled between Shimbashi (Tokyo) and Yokohama, bringing an income to the railway of 400,000 *yen*. The lack of toilet facilities – no one had thought they were necessary – soon caused embarrassment. People had to relieve themselves out of the window if they could not wait until Yokohama – until a fine of 10 *yen* was imposed on offenders. Oddly enough, when lavatories were first introduced, for the third-class passengers in 1889 on the Tōkaidō line, they were in the middle of the carriage and contrary to Western usage the Japanese passenger believed that they were not to be used while the train was in motion. The railway lines in the stations, as a result, looked unspeakable until the companies began to do something about it. Carriages were not heated properly until 1903, and to cope with the severe Japanese winter first- and second-class passengers were issued with hot-water bottles. The hardier or less sensitive third-class passengers did without.

Right: A village street in a silk district near Tokyo: before modernisation each home was used as a nursery for silkworms

44

Chapter 3
The Beginnings of Empire

Japan's attempt to modernise herself was undertaken in self-defence. The example of India and China had shown that if you did not make yourself the equal in all respects of the European powers and the USA, they took you over as a colony or shared you out commercially. This explains the importance of the extra-territoriality issue. The expression refers to the practice, written into the treaties the Western powers made with Japan in the days of the declining and helpless *bakufu,* of insisting on their subjects being tried by their own consular courts for crimes committed in Japan. The practice was imposed everywhere in the East and was symbolic of the Western contempt for Eastern standards of civilisation. It was deeply offensive to Japan's national pride. But there was a case for it as far as the administration of justice was concerned.

'Japan had no known system of law,' wrote a former British consul at Nagasaki, 'no organised courts of justice or competent legal officers; torture was an incident of every criminal trial; the death penalty was daily inflicted for offences against property or persons of the most trivial character; and the prisons were infernos of human suffering.'

From Japan's point of view revision of the unequal treaties which had enforced extra-territorial jurisdiction was vital to her standing among other nations. Unless she could obtain it she was publicly branded as incompetent to exercise the standards of justice which prevailed in the advanced countries of the West. The need to achieve this revision was a leading drive behind the imitation of manners and customs from Europe or the USA.

In some cases, too, the justice administered by representatives of the Western powers was inept. Great Britain employed consuls who knew Japan and the Japanese and had taken trouble to familiarise themselves with local custom — men like Sir Ernest Satow. Other powers, whose commercial interests were tiny in comparison and who could not afford a full-time official, entrusted the execution of their laws to merchants who acted as part-time

Left: The Japanese army besieges Peking in the Boxer Rising

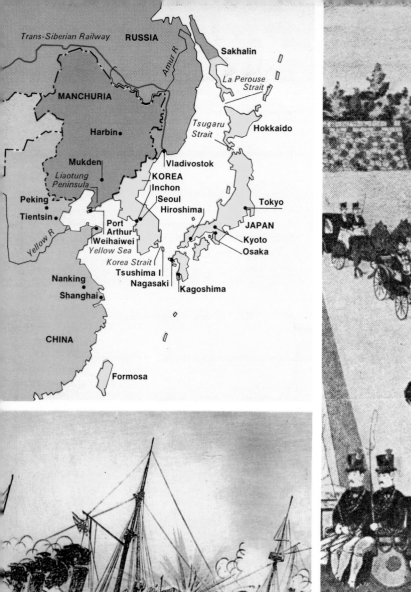

consuls and often had not been properly trained. There was some disadvantage to foreigners themselves, too. They had to live in settlements surrounding the consular courts and could not reside freely where they wished. Iwakura's mission of 1871-3, though successful in many respects, failed to obtain the removal of the unequal treaties. Japan repeated her proposal to abolish extra-territoriality in 1883, after twelve years' laborious work revising the Japanese legal system in the light of Western —particularly French—jurisprudence. Her codes of criminal and civil law were by this time more acceptable, but there was intense opposition from the foreign community to the Japanese proposals.

On the Japanese side there was great resentment when it became known that the Foreign Minister, Inoue, was attempting a compromise in negotiations with the representatives of the Western powers in 1886-7 by offering to set up 'mixed courts' in which foreign judges would sit side by side with Japanese judges when cases involving foreign subjects were heard. The explosion of anger caused by the leakage of these proposals forced Inoue's resignation. An explosion of a more concrete kind nearly put an end to his successor, Ōkuma Shigenobu, whose proposals for treaty revision, though less concessive to the Western powers than Inoue's had been, were still judged to be offensive to Japan's self-esteem. When *The Times* leaked them on 19th April 1889, the government was inundated with protests, and seven months later a youth belonging to the ultra-nationalist Black Ocean Society *(Genyōsha)* threw a bomb at Ōkuma as he was returning from an imperial conference. Ōkuma escaped with his life, but his leg was shattered. The cabinet resigned, and the negotiations were called off.

Finally, in 1894, Great Britain took the lead in accepting the jurisdiction of Japanese courts over British nationals with effect from 1899, on the understanding that the reformed codes would throw open the whole country to foreigners and remove all previous restrictions on trade and travel. Japan had at last achieved the primary task of her foreign policy in the Meiji era: 'It was a proud day for the nation,' wrote one English historian, 'celebrated with public rejoicing such as might have been expected at the close of a long and successful war with a powerful enemy. It was the first experience in history of the unreserved submission of Europeans to the jurisdiction of an oriental state.' Those most directly affected were by no means so enthusiastic and disastrous results

Far left: Japan expands—Formosa was annexed in 1895, Korea in 1910 (top); the Sino-Japanese war—a Japanese battleship in action during the battle of the Yellow Sea (bottom). Left: Departure of the Emperor Meiji for the Imperial GHQ, Hiroshima

were predicted; but they did not occur, and, said one English resident, 'Japan's laws are excellent and her judiciary is just.'

It is a sad comment on the influence of the West that Japan had learned, over the decades, the lesson 'conquer or be conquered'. For she did not hesitate to apply to the prostrate body of Imperial China those very provisions which she had spent so long fighting on her own territory. The ancient, conservative empire of China, and the thrusting, new, westernising empire of Japan came to blows over the country in which they both claimed privileged spheres of interest: Korea.

Korean adventures

Japan's relations with Korea — her *ideas* about Korea, too — have played a crucial part in her foreign policy, both in the distant past and from the Meiji Restoration right up to the present moment. Like most states having a land frontier with China, Korea had been considered as a vassal of the Middle Kingdom and had paid tribute as a token of this; though in the 19th century China was prepared to let Korea negotiate with other countries — Japan, the USA, and Great Britain — as an independent state. The independence was qualified by the presence in the capital, Seoul, of a Chinese resident, who was prepared to back the Korean royal family with force against any wish for change among the Korean people. Some Koreans resented this tutelage and would have preferred to open their country to the West as Japan had done. For others, eager to preserve the status quo, Japan was the progressive enemy, and when riots, provoked by bad rice in military rations, broke out in Seoul in 1882, the blame was laid at the door of the pro-Japanese queen and the Japanese, whose legation was attacked. To make matters worse, the Court refused to allow the Japanese minister, Hanabusa Yoshitada, to take refuge and he had to slip out of the port of Chemulpo (Inchon) at night and seek help from a British ship. The Japanese sent him back with a military and naval escort, and the treaty of Chemulpo was drawn up in 1882 for the payment of reparations and the stationing of Japanese troops in Korea. China sent both troops and ships to Korea to assert her suzerainty, but the Japanese disregarded them and insisted on direct negotiations with Korea.

In 1884 Japanese legation guards were asked to intervene at the Korean royal palace, supposedly under assault by a coup d'état against the queen. The king was withdrawn from the palace by Koreans assisted by Chinese;

Left: The Japanese advance on Port Arthur, November 1894. Their victory surprised the world — and startled the Russians

the Japanese withdrew to Chemulpo after suffering casualties but soon returned with reinforcements under two Japanese generals, who entered Seoul in January 1885. Itō Hirobumi was then sent to China as envoy extraordinary to arrange for the withdrawal of both Japanese and Chinese troops. The Tientsin Treaty was drawn up, Japan and China agreeing to give each other prior notice when either intended to send troops into Korea and to withdraw them when any issue was settled.

The Sino-Japanese war

Ten years later, revolt broke out in Korea and the Korean royal family asked China for help to put it down. 2,500 Chinese troops set up camp at Asan in south-west Korea. Japan was duly notified and decided to send troops herself to the Seoul area as a counterbalance. Referring to Korea as her 'tributary state', China rejected a Japanese proposal to form a union which would bring to an end Korea's grievous maladministration. How could Japan propose this, they inquired, and at the same time assert Korea's independence? After telling China to keep out, Itō sent Japanese troops into the Korean royal palace. China attempted to reinforce her contingent and on 25th July 1894 three of her warships escorting a troop transport fired on two Japanese cruisers, with disastrous results to themselves. The transport and one cruiser were sent to the bottom, another was abandoned, and a third fled. Within a week war was officially declared between Japan and China. It was really too easy: in one month the Japanese army took nearly the whole of Korea. In mid-September eleven Japanese ships encountered a Chinese squadron fourteen strong with two armoured battleships of 7,000 tons. The Japanese sank four Chinese ships, while the rest made for Weihaiwei. Japan, in control of the Yellow Sea, promptly began to reduce the forts on the Liaotung and Shantung Peninsulas: Talien (Dairen), Port Arthur, Weihaiwei. In Weihaiwei the Chinese Admiral Ting fought hard but lost his entire torpedo squadron and then committed suicide. The capture of Weihaiwei ended the war, as a result of which Japan had lost 1,005 men killed and 4,922 wounded from a five-column force of 120,000 men (over 17,000 died of disease), and at a cost of 100,000,000 *yen* (£20,000,000). But her gains were very great: by the peace treaty the Chinese conceded independence to Korea and handed over the island of Formosa, the Pescadores and the Liaotung Peninsula to Japan, in addition to paying a cash indemnity of 200,000,000 *taels*. Japan had successfully joined the wolves of Europe in the game of tearing China to pieces.

Then the rest of the pack turned on her. The European

powers had thought that Japan would be worsted by the immense mass of the Chinese Empire. When the contrary occurred they decided to intervene. The peace treaty of Shimonoseki was signed on 17th April 1895. On 23rd April the ambassadors of Russia, Germany, and France called at the Japanese Foreign Office and presented a memorandum 'recommending' that Japan should return the Liaotung Peninsula to China. They declared that if Japan remained in possession of it she would be a constant threat to Peking, Korea's independence would be a fiction, and the peace of the Far East would be threatened. The German minister was not very subtle. He pointed out that if Japan did not accede to the wishes of the *Dreibund* ('Pact of Three') she could not win. The Japanese Vice-Minister for Foreign Affairs, Hayashi, took umbrage at this and obtained a rewording of the offensive German memorandum. But the facts themselves were hard enough to swallow, however diplomatic the language in which they were couched. A series of conferences in the Emperor's presence was held at the Imperial GHQ in Hiroshima to discuss the memorandum, and finally Japan caved in, because her diplomats had found out that no Western power would back her up if she determined to resist with force. 'Russia seems to be in constant fear,' wrote the Japanese minister in Moscow, 'that her territories would be threatened by land and sea if Japan possessed a powerful strategic harbour in the Liaotung Peninsula. Japan, using the said harbour as a base of operations, could wield her power not only over the peninsula, but also over the whole of Korea as well as the fertile lands of northern Manchuria.' Of the three European powers involved France was merely acting as Russia's European ally, while Germany was attempting to divert Russia's attention from Europe. It was Russia's vital interests that were at stake, and she was prepared to use force to secure them.

The humiliation felt by the Japanese was tremendous. But the lesson was learnt: it was the weak who were humiliated. Her legal system had been accepted, but Japan would remain a second-class power until her military forces gave her the confidence to withstand the pressures of Europe. China had been an easy enemy, and Marshal Yamagata had taken her military measure long before war broke out. China's real army was very small: 50,000 men under Li Hung Chang, the Viceroy of Pechihli, trained by German instructors. In addition there were about a million troops of very questionable value, and of these only 300,000 were in the northern provinces. With 200,000 men at his disposal, Yamagata put aside

Left: Admiral Kabayama, victor in the battle of the Yellow Sea

53

50,000 to cope with Li Hung Chang's army, and another 150,000 to deal with the semi-trained 300,000 in the rest of north China. Even Li Hung Chang's army had a great defect (and it resembled the pre-Meiji Japanese forces in this): both officers and men were drawn from their commander's native place, and replacements for officers had to come from there too, not from other parts of the Chinese 'army'. And it was corrupt. In theory a battalion consisted of 500 men, but the real strength was 300 to 350, the battalion commander pocketing the difference in pay allocated to his '500' by the government. Needless to say, Yamagata did not have to wait for the campaign to start before he knew this. His system of espionage in north China had provided him with an accurate picture of the situation long before, just as, in the case of Russia in 1904, it was to provide him with a precise account of Russian forces in Manchuria.

Russian manoeuvres

There is a certain inevitability about the Russo-Japanese war. For two centuries Russia had been pushing across Asia, and in the 1860s had taken from China the Maritime Province of Siberia, reaching the shores of the Pacific down to the Korean frontier. But the outlets from her new port, Vladivostok, were still straddled by Japan: the narrow Tsugaru Strait between Hokkaidō and Honshu, the La Pérouse Strait between Sakhalin and Hokkaidō, and the Korea Strait which was wider than the other two − 102 miles from shore to shore − but effectively cut into controllable channels by Japan's ownership of the islands of Tsushima and Iki. Russia had seen the importance of Tsushima in 1860, when she sent a ship to found a settlement on the island as a token of ownership. The attempt might have succeeded had Great Britain not intervened to uphold Japan's claim. So Russia still had no ice-free port in the Far East; and the solution offered seemed to be control over Korea, which would permit her to debouch directly into the Yellow Sea. Here lies the real cause of the *Dreibund* intervention of 1895 which prevented Japan holding on to the Liaotung Peninsula.

Russia's Trans-Siberian Railway had to make an enormous northward curve along the line of the Amur frontier of Manchuria, and it was obviously preferable, if a suitable occasion were to present itself, to take the line straight through Harbin to Vladivostok. Ostensibly Russia had 'befriended' China in 1895 against Japan, and her reward was the right to construct her railway, known as the Chinese Eastern Railway, across Man-

Left: Cartoonists' views of international peace − John Bull halts the scramble for China (top), Europe cries 'Enough!' (bottom)

55

churia. Nor did she stop there. When Germany, using the pretext of the murder of two German subjects, demanded from China the cession of Shantung, Russia put pressure on China for a lease of the Liaotung Peninsula, which she obtained – the very shores from which she had managed to extrude Japan in 1895. It needs little imagination to reconstruct the reaction of the Japanese to this bare-faced piece of power politics. Something very similar happened in Peking and Tientsin during the Boxer Rebellion of 1900. Japan's forces of 20,000 men were despatched to save the foreign legations in Shantung Province, at the request of the Western powers, and after the relief of the legations Japan withdrew half her forces immediately. Russia used the same occasion to push garrisons into Manchuria and was soon in virtual possession of the country. It was only a question of time before she would attempt to penetrate into Korea to use the south Korean ports. Japan's stake was considerable. She owned the Korean railway system, and tens of thousands of Japanese had settled in the peninsula. Most of its overseas trade was in Japanese hands.

This time Japan did not lack friends. America and Great Britain were fully aware of the implications of Russia's Manchurian policy and supported Japan in an attempt to make China resist Russia's request for a formal cession of Manchuria. Russia was compelled to agree to withdraw her troops in three stages, all at precise dates.

The signing of the Anglo-Japanese alliance on 30th January 1902 made it possible for Japan to consider military resistance to Russia's demands in Manchuria and Korea. Britain had not agreed to come to Japan's aid automatically, should she become involved in any way with Russia over Korea; but the terms of the alliance made it plain that Britain recognised that Japan had not only commercial and industrial but also political interests in Korea. If either Britain or Japan became engaged in war in Asia – Britain naturally had her Indian north-west frontier with Russia in mind – the other signatory would guarantee to remain neutral if only one enemy were involved; if more than one, then military aid would be forthcoming. Intervention by European powers on Russia's behalf would also be met with hostility by the USA, whose president Theodore Roosevelt was in a very pro-Japanese mood. 'As soon as this war broke out,' he said later of the Russo-Japanese war, 'I notified Germany and France that in the event of a combination against Japan I should promptly side with Japan and proceed to whatever length was necessary on her behalf.'

Far right: The heroes of the Russo-Japanese war – General Nogi (top) and Admiral Tōgō. Right: Crew of a Japanese cruiser

At first it looked as if Russia might take Britain's hint when she began the first phased withdrawal of her troops from the occupied areas of Manchuria. A second, timed for April 1903, did not take place, because at a meeting in February between the Tsar and a number of his ministers the party favouring compromise with Japan and prepared to sacrifice Russian claims to south Manchuria and Korea lost the day. The Tsar decided against the moderates among his advisers and took the unusual step in the summer of 1903 of bypassing his Foreign Minister, Lamsdorff—himself a moderate—and creating a 'Viceroy of the Russian Far East' who was empowered to negotiate direct with China, Korea, and Japan—thus neatly taking the control of Far Eastern affairs completely out of the hands of the Russian Foreign Ministry. The Viceroy was Admiral Eugene Alexeiev, rumoured to be the illegitimate son of the Tsar Alexander II, and an extremist in Asian affairs, who sympathised with the views of the Privy Councillor Ivan Bezobrazov. 'The Far East is still in a period,' Bezobrazov had written, 'when stubborn struggle is necessary in order to assure the consolidation of our realm. Domination by us is the ultimate aim of this struggle. Without such domination we will not be able either to rule the yellow race or control the hostile influence of our European rivals.'

'Korea,' said the Russian envoy to Korea, 'must be Russian.' In pursuance of this policy, the Russian forces in the East were subordinated to a newly formed 'Special Committee for Far Eastern Affairs' headed by Bezobrazov and another extremist, Admiral Abaza. In June 1903 a Japanese Imperial conference proposed terms of settlement with Russia of their joint interests: both would guarantee the territorial integrity of China and Korea; Russia's special railway interests in Manchuria would be recognised, so would Japan's political and economic interests in Korea. In October 1903 Russia replied that she would be prepared to guarantee Korea only, thus making it clear that she had further designs on Manchuria. She also wanted Japan to refrain from fortifying the coast of Korea, as well as to renounce any special interest in Manchuria. It was a considerable rebuff and made war seem probable. Edward VII of England attempted to mediate in November 1903, but without success. Japan repeated her terms in January 1904 and the Japanese ambassador made it plain in St Petersburg that they were, in effect, an ultimatum.

The Tsar telegraphed to his Viceroy on 8th February 1904 that it was desirable that the Japanese and not the

*Top right: Japanese Red Cross workers treating wounded Russians. **Bottom:** A Japanese naval gun in the battle of Tsushima*

58

大日本赤十字衞生隊
戰闘中ノ負傷者救護之圖

Russians should be seen to start hostilities. 'But,' he went on, 'if their army should cross the 38th parallel on the west coast of Korea, without a landing, you are hereby given discretion to attack them without waiting for the first shot from their side.' The Japanese did not trouble to go through the formality of declaring war – at first. On 8th February ten Japanese destroyers attacked the Russian squadron at Port Arthur. They delivered their torpedoes, holed two battleships and a cruiser, and returned undamaged across the moonlit sea to their port of Sasebo. The next day, Japanese battleships under their commander-in-chief Admiral Tōgō shelled the Russian squadron and forced it to withdraw into the harbour of Port Arthur. At the same time Admiral Uryu's squadron, escorting Japanese troop transports to Chemulpo, the port of Seoul, ordered a Russian gunboat and a transport to stand out to sea or be shelled where they lay. The Russians came out and were so badly damaged in the battle which followed that their crews took the ships back into port and scuttled them. War was declared on 10th February 1904, but these sharp defeats of Russia's naval forces had already set the stage for what was to happen.

The Russo-Japanese war

The Japanese strategy was to destroy Russia's naval strength in the Pacific, so that Japan could have freedom of action in transporting her troops to any spot on the continent she chose. Part of her armies was to take Port Arthur on the tip of the Liaotung Peninsula, while the main body pushed into Manchuria through Liaoyang and Mukden. Russian forces at the beginning were numerically inferior to the Japanese, though at sea they were roughly equal. The Russians planned to avoid a full-scale battle until the Japanese army, halted by nothing more than skirmishing delays, should be drawn into the Manchurian interior with extended lines of communication. The Russians would concentrate at Liaoyang on giving battle, and if that was not decisive Harbin would see the coup de grâce.

Within three months of war being declared Japan had landed her armies in Korea and pushed them across the Yalu into Manchuria. There, on 18th April 1904, they defeated 20,000 Russians under General Zasulich. The Third Army under General Nogi laid siege to Port Arthur on 6th June. It was well fortified and stubbornly defended and the Japanese paid a heavy price – 20,000 dead – for their inch by inch advance. Inexorably they closed in, and on 1st January 1905 the Russian commander, Stössel, surrendered 878 officers, 23,491 men, over 500 guns, more than 35,000 rifles, 2,250,000 rounds of am-

munition, four battleships, two cruisers, fourteen gun-
boats, and many other smaller vessels.

This massive victory released Nogi's forces for the
march on Mukden, which Field-Marshal Ōyama, the
Supreme Japanese Commander in Manchuria, realised
he must make sure of with speed, since his Russian opposite number, Prince Kuropatkin, was gradually build-
ing up his forces to 500,000 men with troops pouring into
Siberia from Europe. In the battle for Mukden the Japanese now had sixteen divisions—about 250,000 men—
facing 320,000 Russians over a 50-mile front. The struggle
between these vast forces lasted for over three weeks
(20th February—16th March 1905) and on 10th March
the Japanese took the city of Mukden, at a loss of over
40,000 men—one half of the Russian losses. This battle,
which a Japanese historian considers to be one of the
decisive battles of history, put paid to any thoughts the
Russians may have had of victory. It also taught foreign
military observers the quality of the Japanese staff. They
had already seen the stubborn bravery of the Japanese
infantry under fire, in battles like that of Kinchou in
which 10,000 Russians held a dominating position,
strongly defended by fifty siege guns. The Japanese took
it by frontal assault, at great cost. 'With almost everything in its favour,' wrote the military correspondent of
The Times, 'a strong, fresh, and confident Russian army,
solidly entrenched behind almost inaccessible fortifica-
tions and supported by a formidable and superior artillery,
was, in a single day, swept out of its trenches.' The battle
of Mukden showed something more than sheer bravery.
The military attachés of foreign armies witnessed a
Japanese staff launching, directing, and maintaining
a quarter of a million men over a vast front in a country
with poor communications. It was a feat of which any
European army would have been proud.

Russia did not surrender on the loss of this most important land battle. She still thought she might redress
the balance at sea, where her losses had already been
considerable. Perhaps Japan might still be blockaded
and supplies to her armies on the Asian continent cut off
by a vast naval operation. On 16th October 1904 the
Russian Baltic fleet under Admiral Rozhdestvensky had
left Kronstadt to sail round the world. The only fleet with
enough coaling stations to do this successfully had been
thought to be the British; but French ports in Madagascar
and Indo-China helped the Russian ships on, and by
May 1905 they were in the Pacific. Admiral Tōgō was sure
the Russians would take the short cut to Vladivostok

Left: *President Theodore Roosevelt, shown with the Japanese
delegate, was the mediator in the negotiations with Russia*

through the Tsushima Strait and his scouts sighted them off Quelpart Island at 5 am on 27th May. By sunset of that day the fate of the Russian Baltic Fleet was sealed. The flagship and three other battleships had been sent to the bottom, one admiral had been killed and another wounded. The third admiral surrendered the following day. By the end of this two-day running battle in the Sea of Japan, the Russians had lost six battleships, five cruisers, and several destroyers and smaller craft. Of 18,000 sailors, only 6,000 survived. The Japanese lost 116 men killed and three torpedo boats. It was a naval victory on a colossal scale.

From start to finish the war had been a disaster for the Russian government. 'We need a small victorious war,' the Minister of the Interior had said, 'to stem the tide of revolution.' The defeat helped to bring the revolutionaries out into the streets of St Petersburg, where they were shot down in their hundreds. It was little wonder that Lenin saw in Japan's victory the seeds of Russia's future revolution.

The combatants were brought to the conference table by President Theodore Roosevelt at Portsmouth, New Hampshire, where the peace treaty was signed on 5th September 1905. Japan's paramount interests in Korea were recognised; both Russia and Japan would evacuate Manchuria at the same time; Russia's lease of the Liaotung Peninsula from China would be taken over by Japan; so would the Russian railway south of Kwangchengtsz, with the mining rights that went with it; the southern half of the island of Sakhalin was to go to Japan; Japanese fishermen were granted rights in the Okhotsk and Bering Seas; both powers pledged themselves not·to exploit Manchurian railways for strategic ends. All parts of occupied Manchuria were to be returned to Chinese administration, except for leased territory, and Russia had to disavow any ambition to secure a monopoly of privileges or concessions in China. She refused, though, to pay the indemnity Japan had demanded, and Japan withdrew this clause.

Russian information had it – correctly – that Japan was on the brink of financial exhaustion and Russia felt she could afford to stiffen her attitude. But Japan's concession on this point had repercussions at home. Riots broke out in Tokyo when it became known that Japan would receive nothing from Russia in the way of indemnity after her immense sacrifices. The force of angry public opinion unseated Prince Katsura's cabinet which had successfully concluded the war, and in January 1906 it resigned.

Left: The Emperor Meiji reviews his troops in a victory parade. The coachman bears the full trappings of European ceremonial

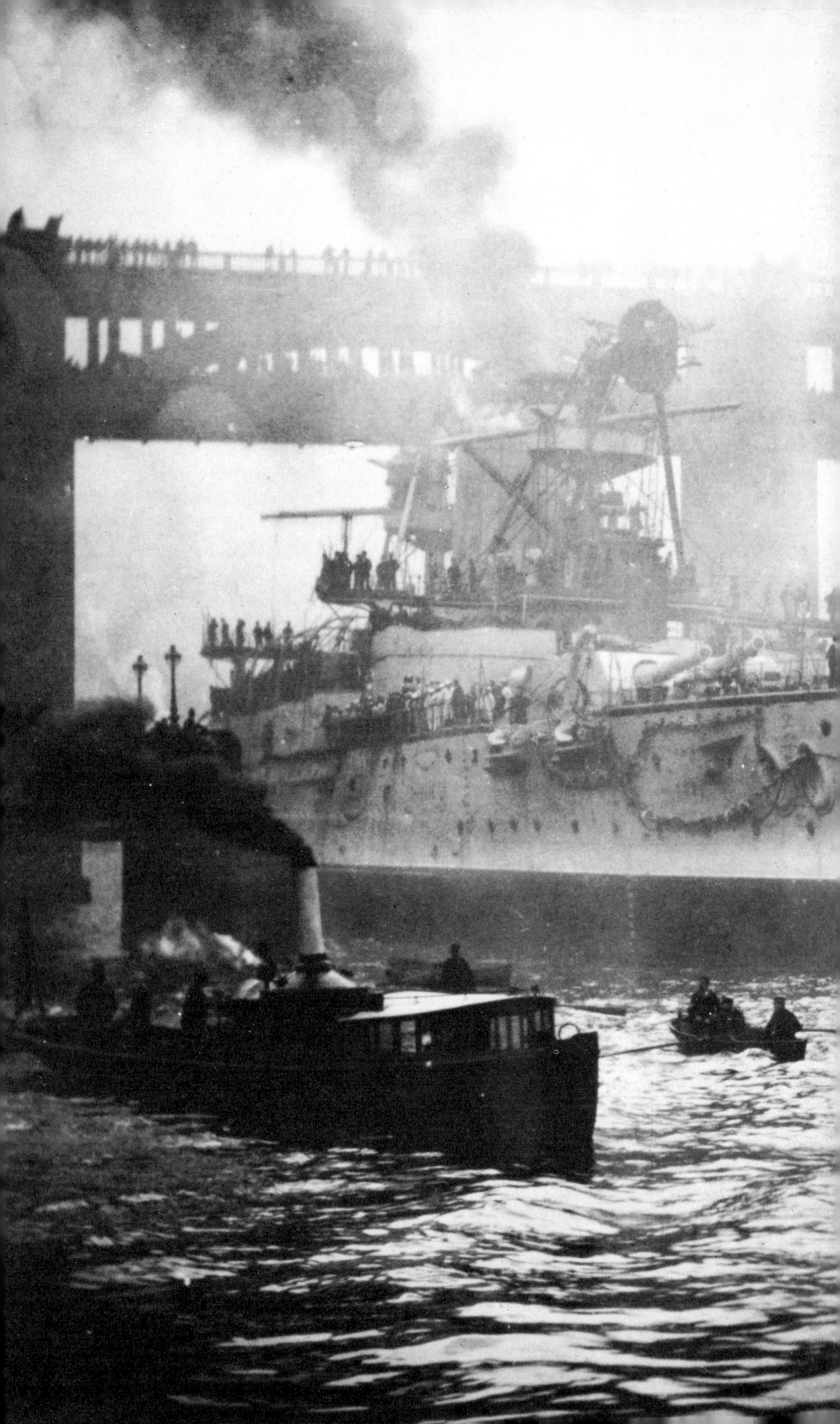

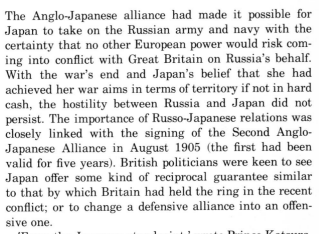

Chapter 4
Japan's Gains in the First World War

The Anglo-Japanese alliance had made it possible for Japan to take on the Russian army and navy with the certainty that no other European power would risk coming into conflict with Great Britain on Russia's behalf. With the war's end and Japan's belief that she had achieved her war aims in terms of territory if not in hard cash, the hostility between Russia and Japan did not persist. The importance of Russo-Japanese relations was closely linked with the signing of the Second Anglo-Japanese Alliance in August 1905 (the first had been valid for five years). British politicians were keen to see Japan offer some kind of reciprocal guarantee similar to that by which Britain had held the ring in the recent conflict; or to change a defensive alliance into an offensive one.

'From the Japanese standpoint,' wrote Prince Katsura, 'the nation needed a period of recuperation after the Russo-Japanese War, and the possibility of a Russian revenge could not be precluded [the British Foreign Secretary Lord Lansdowne had been at pains to stress this point]. By concluding a firm alliance with Great Britain, Japan would be able to rebuild her strength and heal the scars of war.' So in the terms of the Second Anglo-Japanese Alliance, Great Britain and Japan each promised to come to the other's help if either were attacked by a third party without provocation. Great Britain obtained what she wanted: the possibility of removing Russian pressure from the frontiers of India by the inclusion of references to India in the East Asia area envisaged by the treaty. And Japan gave Britain notice, in the last of three secret articles of her first draft, that she intended to take over Korea, which was annexed in 1910.

Britain now recognised Japan's paramount political, military, and economic interest in Korea and acknowledged 'the right of Japan to take such measures of guidance, control, and protection in Korea as she may deem proper and necessary to safeguard and advance those interests' provided Japan guaranteed equal trade

Left: A newly-built Japanese battleship leaves the Tyne, 1914

opportunities to other nations. The Alliance was to run for ten years. When Sir Charles Hardinge, the British ambassador in St Petersburg, revealed the terms to the Russian Foreign Minister, Lamsdorff (rather naturally) replied that his government was bound to view it as directed against Russia, and could hardly be expected to welcome it. But Lamsdorff was replaced by Iswolsky after the defeat of 1905 and Russia's attitude began to change. Like Witte, the Russian Minister of Finance, Iswolsky — once Russia's envoy to Japan — had belonged to a group which favoured a rapprochement with the Japanese, and he even considered the Treaty of Portsmouth as favourable to Russia herself, because it ultimately paved the way to a Russo-Japanese agreement. A short-lived attempt to draw closer to Germany proved fruitless, and so Russia, allied as she was with France, embarked on a policy of reaching an agreement with Great Britain. As a result of the closer ties with France and England, Russia was coaxed, in spite of her extremists, into a more understanding frame of mind in relation to Japan. A Franco-Japanese agreement was signed in 1907, making the usual polite sounds about respecting the integrity of China while mapping out mutually agreed spheres of influence, Japan agreeing for her part to respect France's territorial rights in Indo-China. Watching Japan build up a network of alliances, Russia gradually followed suit with a number of agreements on Manchurian railways and fishing rights in the Sea of Okhotsk in 1907, the first Russo-Japanese agreement being signed in June of that year, with a second agreement following in July 1910. As a mutual response to an American attempt to intervene in the Manchurian railway system, a third agreement was signed in 1912. The Third Anglo-Japanese Alliance was concluded, four years before the second was due to expire, in July 1911, in spite of growing hostility by sections of the British press to what was interpreted as Japan's threat to Britain's commercial interests in China. The spinning of this web of alliances and agreements more or less dictated Japan's course on the outbreak of war in Europe in the summer of 1914.

Not at once, though. There was some fear among the Allies that Japan might be attracted towards Germany, since many of her elder statesmen, like the old marshal Yamagata, had a healthy respect for German arms and thought a German victory was quite on the cards; in addition Prince Itō, who had been assassinated by a Korean fanatic in Harbin five years previously, had im-

Right: Japan's military role in the First World War was limited to seizing German possessions in China and the Pacific: troops preparing for action (top), and advancing on Tsingtao (bottom)

66

parted to his followers, now powerful in Japan's government, a deep respect for the German state. At first Britain hoped to keep Japan out of the war, but on 7th August 1914 she felt compelled to invoke Japan's aid, under the terms of the Alliance, against German commerce-raiders in Far Eastern waters. The Foreign Minister, Katō, pointed out to the cabinet that although no conditions existed whereby Japan had to go to war, it would be a friendly gesture to Britain and an opportunity to take over German possessions in China and the Pacific. Having made the decision to go to war the Japanese government was taken aback when Great Britain pointed out that she had hoped only for protection of commerce at sea and asked Japan to hold her declaration of war in abeyance. This the Japanese refused to do and their ultimatum was sent on 15th August demanding the withdrawal of German naval vessels from Japanese and Chinese waters, as well as the surrender of the leased territory of Kiaochow.

Germany sent no reply and Japan declared war on 23rd August. In under three months she had taken all German possessions on the Chinese mainland as well as the Marshalls, the Marianas, and the Carolines. Apart from convoy duty in the Indian Ocean and the despatch of destroyers to the Mediterranean, Japan intervened no further in the European war as a combatant. Her cabinet refused troops for the Western Front on the grounds that to send an expeditionary force of any useful size to Europe would seriously weaken her at home. She also had no intention of being distracted from China.

Japan's 'Twenty-one Demands'

In 1914 China had been a republic for two years, after Sun Yat Sen's revolution against the Manchu dynasty in 1911. Sun Yat Sen was friendly to Japan and had lived there as an exile. He did not become China's first president, though — this fell to Yuan Shih K'ai, who had been a functionary under the Manchus and against whom Sun led a revolt in 1913. Ill-treatment of Japanese in Nanking spurred the Japanese government to put pressure on Yuan in an attempt to overthrow him, but when in 1914 Ōkuma Shigenobu became Prime Minister he preferred diplomatic methods. His cabinet worked out a series of 'Twenty-one Demands' as a follow-up to Japan's take-over of German territories in China. These were presented to Peking in January 1915. The 'Demands' were in five groups:

Right: Japan's excessive ambitions in China turned American public opinion against her. This American cartoon celebrates the confirmation in 1917 of the traditional Open Door policy in China, but Japan now took on the role of bully

i Four articles on the disposition of German economic rights in Shantung

ii Seven articles strengthening Japan's position in South Manchuria and Eastern Inner Mongolia

iii Two articles to secure mining and railway concessions in Central China

iv One article forbidding China to lease or cede any harbour, bay, or island on the Chinese coast to a third power

v Seven 'requests', intended to make China accept Japanese advisers in a number of military and financial organisations.

Some of the Demands were those of a strong nation putting pressure on a weaker: the extension of the lease on Port Arthur, Dairen, the South Manchurian Railway, and the Antung-Mukden Railway from twenty-five to ninety-nine years, for example. Others were of the kind no self-respecting power could accept and still hope to retain a vestige of independence: police administration in all important Chinese towns to be under Japanese control, consultation with Japan before foreign capital could be invested in mining, railway, or harbour projects in Fukien Province, Japan's veto over the employment of foreign nationals in Manchuria and Inner Mongolia. The fifth group, the 'requests', was withdrawn during negotiation and slight modifications were made in the rest. Then the Japanese presented them again in a peremptory manner in April 1915, and on 9th May China gave in. It was a humiliating surrender for a sovereign state. And the Demands were in radical contradiction to Ōkuma's own statement in August 1914: 'Japan has no ulterior motive, no desire to secure more territory, no thought of depriving China or other peoples of anything which they now possess.'

The Demands caused great resentment among world opinion, particularly in America, though the *Washington Times* declared that 'Asia is Japan's natural field of enterprise.' Then complaints began to flow into the State Department from Americans in China of discrimination against them in many fields of business, and relations became strained. When the USA went to war in 1917, Japan used the opportunity to send a mission under Viscount Ishii to restore friendship. With Lansing, the Secretary of State, he drew up an agreement reaffirming the Open Door policy — 'equal opportunity for commerce and industry in China'. The preamble of the agreement was interesting: 'The Governments of the United States

Left: Japanese troops remained in Siberia till 1922, lending support to anti-Soviet leaders and meeting brutality with brutality in a manner that would have appalled General Nogi

71

and Japan recognise that territorial propinquity creates special relations between countries, and consequently the Government of the United States recognises that Japan has special interests in China, particularly in the part to which her possessions are contiguous.'

The statement was susceptible of a wide variety of interpretations. Lansing, and the American public at large, took the terms to recognise the facts of geography. The Japanese took them as an American admission of Japan's special influence in China, though Lansing pointed out at a later inquiry that Ishii had wanted the words 'and influence' inserted after 'special interests' but had agreed to strike them out at Lansing's request.

It was not intended to endorse the Twenty-one Demands. It seems not improbable that American and Japanese business interests were preparing joint ventures in China, which the American community in China did not welcome, and because of this split American opinion reacted in a rather ambiguous fashion.

The Bolshevik Revolution of 1917 complicated matters still further. The Allied governments wished to prevent released prisoners from the Central Powers spreading into the Far East, and to help the Czechs among them who, not wishing to join the Soviets, were retreating eastwards along the Trans-Siberian Railway. A military intervention was proposed, Japan being the first of the Allied powers to send forces into the troubled areas. At the same time Japan felt she and China should act together, and by a secret Agreement for Common Defence made in May 1918 Japanese commanders took control of Chinese troops operating into Russian territory from China. Japanese contingents remained in Siberia until 1922, supporting by their presence some highly dubious anti-Soviet elements and behaving with a violence that contrasted with the chivalry which had so impressed Western observers during the Russo-Japanese War of 1904-5.

Effects of the First World War

The First World War brought great economic benefits to Japan. Her population had increased by one quarter between 1895 and 1914 (from 41,000,000 to over 52,000,000) but her farms and fishing fleets had kept her people fed, with the aid of imported foodstuffs. The rice crop went up by one third and her foreign trade doubled

Right: Crown Prince Hirohito rides through a Tokyo devastated by the most severe earthquake in Japan in modern times. Old superstition held that a giant catfish lived underground which, when stirred by the chronic folly of the men who lived above, would heave his back in anger. In the earthquake of 1923 all Yokohama was destroyed, and over half of Tokyo

between 1893 and 1903. Between 1893 and 1914 her consumption of coal increased sevenfold, and railway mileage by a factor of three. Two wars had already given a great fillip to her merchant marine (it doubled in two years as a result of the needs of the Sino-Japanese War). Her total industrial production, in the quarter of a century ending in 1914, had risen by nearly 100 per cent. War brought its disadvantages, of course. Japan lost 120,000 tons of shipping to attacks by German raiders; but in 1913 she had 1,500,000 tons, and her government-subsidised shipyards turned out 50,000 tons a year.

Europe's inability to supply overseas markets when her industries were locked in war was Japan's opportunity. Asia was an apparently bottomless market, and Japan had the textiles it needed. Three-quarters of her cotton goods went to China, including Hong Kong and the Kwantung Leased Territories, two-thirds of her raw silk to the USA. Between 1914 and 1918 exports of cotton cloth rose by 185 per cent. By the end of the war her merchant fleet had nearly doubled in tonnage, and its income – with the increase in freight rates – rose from 41,000,000 *yen* in 1914 to over 381,000,000 *yen* in 1919 – nearly a tenfold increase. The number of workers employed in factories doubled, and manufacturing output rose by three-quarters.

Prices soared too, and the urban population felt the impact of this: there were riots in several Japanese cities in 1918 because wages were not keeping pace with the rise in prices. Not all Japanese profited equally from the wartime trade boom. There was considerable industrial unrest in 1918 and 1919 and although strikes were illegal many workers – railwaymen, postmen, schoolteachers – came out in support of wage claims.

Domestic unrest

The increase in industrialisation resulting from the contracts of the First World War did not bring permanent prosperity to Japan's countryside. During the war farmers had been well paid for their rice, when its price in the cities tripled in one twelve-month period. The rise continued into the post-war period, and a *koku* of rice which cost 16 *yen* in 1917 cost 55 *yen* in 1920. In a single year this price was then halved, so that many of the poorer farmers lost half their income. Many of them did not own or rent a plot of land big enough to permit a variety of crop to cushion themselves against loss: nearly half Japan's farms were 1½ acres in size, or even less. Agricultural discontent and trades union militancy – there were 200 unions by 1920 – fused together in 1925 and 1926 in an attempt to achieve in the Diet representation of the interests of peasants and city workers, as the pro-

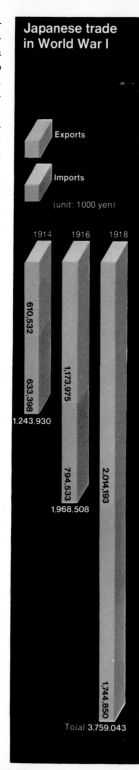

Japanese trade in World War I

Exports

Imports

(unit: 1000 yen)

	1914	1916	1918
Exports	610,532	1,173,975	2,014,193
Imports	633,398	794,533	1,744,850
Total	1,243,930	1,968,508	3,759,043

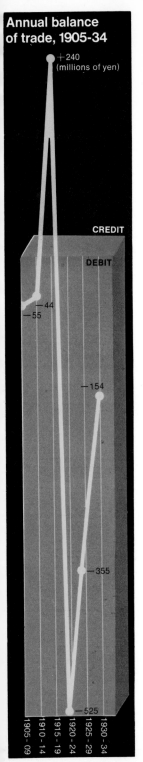

+240
(millions of yen)

CREDIT

DEBIT

—44
—55

—154

—355

—525

1905 - 09
1910 - 14
1915 - 19
1920 - 24
1925 - 29
1930 - 34

perty qualification for the vote was abolished in 1925.

The Farmer-Labour Party, *Nōmin-Rōdōtō*, was formed, and promptly banned. Its less extreme successor, the Labour-Farmer Party, *Rōdō-Nōmintō*, soon split as the result of internal dissensions. As if their own domestic squabbles were not enough the left-wing parties suffered from the same kind of police persecution which had harried the growth of the Liberal Party and the Constitutional Party in the 1880s, with the additional hazard that police regulations decreed in 1925 could ensure long prison sentences for members of any society whose aim was to abolish private ownership.

Great wealth side by side with poverty, rice riots, industrial strikes, police persecution, political murder—the violence which is never far below the surface in Japanese life began to play a more open and conspicuous role in politics as militarism and nationalism grew throughout the twenties and early thirties. Japanese politicians in the past had both used—and been the victims of—the threat or reality of assassination. Okubo Toshimichi, one of the most gifted of the early Meiji leaders, had been murdered in 1878, Itagaki had been stabbed in 1882, the Queen of Korea had been killed by a Japanese in 1895, Prince Itō had died at the hands of a Korean fanatic in Harbin in 1909, Ōkuma Shigenobu had lost a leg in a bomb attempt upon his life in 1889. These events might be put down to the growing pains of a new society. But even in the more democratic Japan of the 1920s violence and assassination were customary weapons. Fomented partly by secret political societies whose aim was to promote Japanese expansion into Asia, partly by groupings of fanatical army officers, the control of the military over Japanese life was gradually strengthened from the end of the twenties.

Left: The massive expansion of the Japanese wartime economy

Chapter 5
The Twenties: Army Misrule

With the death of Field Marshal Yamagata in 1922, the elder statesmen of the Meiji oligarchy had all disappeared from the political scene with the exception of the last *genrō*, or Imperial adviser, Prince Saionji, who survived until 1940. The firm control from the Imperial throne, which had been exercised until 1912 by the Emperor Meiji, could not be expected either from the mentally incapable son who succeeded him as the Emperor Taishō or from the young Prince Regent Hirohito who took over from his father in 1921 and succeeded to the throne in 1926. The two major parties, both of a vaguely conservative-liberal tinge, *Seiyūkai* (Society of Political Friends) and *Kenseikai* (Constitutional Party), were closely linked with the increasingly ramified power of the *zaibatsu* (big business combines) Mitsui and Mitsubishi. The *Kenseikai* had been founded in 1915, with the Foreign Minister Katō Takaaki as its president, to act as an opposition to the military and the elder statesmen. It became the *Minseitō* (Democratic Party) in the mid-twenties. The *Seiyūkai* relied for support on conservative rural elements in Japan; the *Minseitō* looked more to the cities and to business. In the outbursts of army officers against democratic party government during the next decade, hatred for politicians of these parties was linked with the resolution to destroy the capitalist structure behind them. One of these military groupings, *Sakura-kai* (the Cherry Society), formed in 1930, spoke in its prospectus with contempt for the politicians who had betrayed Japan in the London Treaty in 1930:

'When we observe the London Treaty, it is evident that the poisonous sword of the demoralised and covetous party politician is about to be turned towards the military. Those of us who are the rank and file of the army must strengthen unity and not only prevent the repetition of the navy's failure, but also with a strong patriotic fervour be ready to wash out the bowels of the corrupt and covetous men who rule us.'

The scornful reference to 'the navy's failure' needs

Left: Baron Wakatsuki signs the London Treaty, St James's 1930

77

some explanation. The London Treaty was a confirmation of the results of earlier negotiations on the naval strengths of the great powers, arrived at during the Washington Conference of 1921.

After the war Japan had done reasonably well out of the Versailles Treaty. She took over Germany's Pacific Islands north of the Equator and the German-leased territory in Shantung. But in a less tangible sphere, that of prestige and self-respect, she suffered a setback which had serious repercussions. Japan's representatives at Versailles wanted the Peace Conference to declare itself unequivocally for racial equality in the new world that was being built. The heated opposition of the Australian representative, Hughes, put paid to this. 'If race equality is recognised in the preamble or any of the articles of the Covenant,' he stormed to Lloyd George, 'I and my people will leave the Conference bag and baggage.' The implications of this decision for Japan and the whole of Asia were, of course, quite unacceptable. And the situation was exacerbated five years later when the USA passed an Immigration Act directed against the immigration of Japanese labour into California.

Prestige was also an issue at the Washington Conference of 1921, which fixed the permissible battleship tonnage of the great naval powers, the USA, Great Britain, and Japan. At first Japan held out for a 10:10:7 ratio, but accepted 5:5:3 provided that the USA and Great Britain agreed to construct no first-class naval bases anywhere closer to Japan than Hawaii, Australia, and Singapore. By its exclusion of Hong Kong, Manila, and Guam from any new fortification programme, this gave Japan mastery of the seas in the Western Pacific. In London, nine years later, the Navy Minister of Hamaguchi's *Minseitō* cabinet continued to accept the 5:5:3 ratio — 'the navy's failure' — in the face of protests from the naval chief-of-staff, who later declared that as far as he was concerned the war against America began from that moment.

The Anglo-Japanese Alliance also went overboard at the Washington Conference, since Great Britain felt in deference to opinion in the USA and Canada that she could not renew it on its old terms, which were held to contradict the letter, if not the spirit, of the League of Nations Covenant and the international disarmament which should ultimately flow from it. Some British politicians understandably regretted its disappearance. However politically wise the move may have appeared at the time, wrote Lord Chatfield, 'we had weakened most gravely our

Right: A German cartoon of the late 1920s disputes Japan's claims to be acting in China for the protection of her citizens

Imperial position. We had turned a powerful friend into a potential and powerful foe.' Japan would have preferred the Alliance to continue, and was not in the least impressed by the empty Four-Power Pact (the USA, Britain, France, Japan) which took its place and offered joint consultation instead of friendship. The Anglo-Japanese Alliance finally came to an end in August 1923.

The Washington Conference also resulted in the Nine-Power Treaty of February 1922 which dealt with China and declared both for China's territorial integrity and for the principle of equal commercial opportunity for all nations. The Chinese also insisted on the unconditional restoration of Shantung, but under British and American pressure reached an agreement with Japan to safeguard Japan's economic supremacy and political influence in the province. As a further step towards friendly relations with China, the Japanese cancelled the Lansing-Ishii Agreement in December 1922. The key figure in these negotiations was Baron Shidehara Kijurō (1872-1951), Japan's chief delegate to the Conference, Foreign Minister of the *Kenseikai* cabinet of 1924-7, and a member of the cabinet of its successor party, the *Minseitō,* from 1929 to 1931. (He survived to become Prime Minister in the early days of the MacArthur regime, 1945-6.) Six months after the Shantung Treaty came into force, Japan promised to return the leased territory of Kiaochow, to withdraw guards posted at Tsingtao within thirty days and also—in six months—the troops who guarded the Kiaochow-Tsinan railway. On 18th January 1927 four principles governing Japan's attitude to China were delivered in the Diet by Shidehara—they consequently became known as the 'Shidehara Policy':

   i Japan would respect China's territorial integrity and refrain from interfering in her domestic affairs

   ii Economic solidarity between the two countries would be encouraged

   iii Japan would show sympathy towards the declared aims of China's government

   iv Japan's essential rights would be protected, while patience would be shown towards China's difficulties.

China was in a condition of constant turbulence owing to Chiang Kai-shek's uneven success in imposing Kuomintang rule and also to his failure in preventing the

Right: Extremist societies flourished in the hothouse atmosphere of the twenties. Violence characterised the activities of the 'Amur River Society': a would-be assassin is led away by detectives (right); members pray—successfully—for the dismissal of an 'unpatriotic' university professor (top right), and parade fully armed before the Imperial Palace (bottom right)

violence of the Kuomintang forces on their way north in 1927, when the foreign communities in Nanking and Hankow were threatened by them. The British would have liked armed intervention to safeguard their interests and people, but Shidehara felt Japan should not send troops. He was concerned with maintaining Japan's economic advance in China—Japan's natural export market—and he did not wish it to be compromised by becoming involved in China's civil war. Earlier still, in 1925, he had refused on two occasions to help the Manchurian warlord Chang Tso Lin against dissident Chinese generals, even though members of his own cabinet urged him to do so in order to protect peace in Manchuria.

Japanese plans for Manchuria

It is doubtful whether Shidehara's policy of wanting the whole of China, not just Manchuria, to welcome economic penetration by Japan would have been successful in the long run. The very force of nationalism that drove the armies of Chiang Kai-shek would ultimately bring them into conflict with Japanese interests in Manchuria which were incompatible with it, even though Chiang Kai-shek visited Japan in 1927 and told the Prime Minister, Tanaka, that if Japan helped the Kuomintang to achieve its aims Japanese interests would be respected.

The *Minseitō* cabinet in which Shidehara was Foreign Minister fell in April 1927, partly as a result of popular resentment against what was termed his 'softness' towards China. It was followed by the Tanaka cabinet, of which the Prime Minister, Tanaka Giichi, was both president of the *Seiyūkai* and a high-ranking general. Both his party and his army affiliations impelled Tanaka to reverse Shidehara's policy of friendliness, and in a single year (1927-8) he sent three expeditions to China to protect Japanese nationals and, incidentally, to stop the civil war spreading into Manchuria. Tanaka's policy was outlined at the Far Eastern Conference in June 1927, at which he was careful to distinguish policy in China from that in Manchuria, because in the latter Japan had a 'special obligation' to maintain order. He had other motives too. As Vice-Chief of the General Staff, Tanaka had advocated the Siberian Expedition of 1917, and since then had dreamed of creating a *cordon sanitaire* in Manchuria and Korea to prevent the spread of communism in East Asia. The seats gained by the reconstituted Japanese Communist Party in the 1928 elections prompted him to similar vigilance at home; in March of that year he arrested over 1,000 communists and left-wing radicals.

Tanaka's plans for separating Manchuria from China had depended on continuing an old policy of support for

the warlord Chang Tso Lin, who ruled Manchuria with the help of the Japanese army. It was to subdue him that Chiang Kai-shek marched north in 1927, because Chang Tso Lin had gradually extended his domain outside Manchuria into north China proper; and as he grew more ambitious, he became more and more restive at Japanese intervention. Tanaka therefore planned to have the Kwantung Army (the Japanese army in Manchuria, so called from the name of the peninsula on which Port Arthur stands) disarm Chang Tso Lin's forces, while at the same time intimating, through the Japanese envoy to Peking, that if Chang withdrew into Manchuria no attempt to disarm him would be made. In this way Tanaka hoped to bring about a situation in which Chang Tso Lin ruled Manchuria under the Japanese umbrella, as before, while the rest of China went to Chiang Kai-shek. When the Kwantung Army heard that Chang was to be permitted to withdraw into Manchuria from north China they were furious. They had thought Tanaka's orders to disarm him showed a strong line in Japanese policy. Frustrated by what seemed to them last-minute weakness, a group of officers took matters into their own hands. On 4th June 1928 Chang Tso Lin's train was blown up by Japan's Independent Railway Guards, under the authority of a Kwantung Army colonel.

The inquiry which followed clearly indicated the complicity of a number of high-ranking army officers, but Tanaka's cabinet pressed him not to court-martial them. Eventually attempts were made to hush the matter up by preferring charges of dereliction of duty against the offenders, including the commanding general of the Kwantung Army. When Tanaka reported this to the Emperor his explanations were cut short and the Emperor refused him further audience. The cabinet fell, and Hamaguchi returned as premier with Shidehara once more as foreign minister. Far from having achieved their aim of involving Japan in a military adventure, the Kwantung Army extremists had merely brought about the return of a 'soft' policy.

The army was undeterred. Assassination proved to be catching, and in Japan it had struck against both party politicians and capitalists. The head of the Yasuda combine, Yasuda Zenjirō, had been struck down in his own home by a right-wing fanatic in 1921. Hara Kei, ex-journalist and foreign ministry official and the first commoner to become prime minister, was killed in the same year. The Prime Minister Hamaguchi was shot and wounded in November 1930 by a member of the *Aikoku-sha,* an ultra-patriotic organisation which favoured vigor-

Left: The ritualisation of violence — learning the martial arts ous expansion on the Asian mainland; he died later of his wounds. His Finance Minister, Inoue Junnosuke, was assassinated in 1932; so was a later prime minister, Inukai Tsuyoshi, in the same year. It became clear that the army was intending a coup d'état to set up a military dictatorship and was prepared to use terror to have its way. The army officers behind these plans modelled themselves, ostensibly, on the clansmen who had overthrown the Tokugawa in 1868, and declared that they would repeat the pattern of national resurgence by creating a *'Shōwa* Restoration' to match the Meiji Restoration. In the spring of 1931 a conspiracy was mounted to achieve this aim and to create a military government headed by the War Minister, General Ugaki. It was only Ugaki's belated withdrawal from the scheme that made it misfire, but a bad example of indiscipline among senior officers had already been set and the way pointed to further violence.

Political corruption: military violence

The chief political parties, the *Seiyūkai* and the *Minseitō*, which alternated in government in the decade 1921-31, proved incapable of controlling these outbursts. For one thing the link between big business and political corruption—one of the targets of the military—was only too well-known. Many of the top-ranking politicians had family connections with the *zaibatsu*. Shidehara's wife, for instance, was an Iwasaki and so directly connected with Mitsubishi. So also was the wife of one of his predecessors, Katō Takaaki. Bribery was known to be used as a means of achieving political ends, whether on a large scale involving international companies, like the naval armaments scandal under the Yamamoto cabinet as far back as 1914, or speculation on land values by both parties in the 1920s. Even the civilian politicians themselves did not despise a heady aura of violence. Hara Kei, *Seiyūkai* premier from 1918 to 1921, used to surround himself with a bodyguard of swashbucklers just like any American ward boss. And Tanaka, as head of the *Seiyūkai*, was quite prepared to connive at military expansionism in Manchuria. But it would be wrong to view all the major figures of the parliamentary parties in the 1920s as pusillanimous: Katō Takaaki, for example, head of the *Kenseikai* (later *Minseitō*), was Prime Minister in 1925 and clearly saw the need to extend the narrow basis of electoral suffrage. He abolished property qualification, and immediately quadrupled the electorate. It was Katō, too, who had the rare courage to attack military expenditure and succeeded in cutting its budget by one quarter; a notable achievement which cost the army four divisions and earned for him its undying hatred. By and large,

though, the parties were not run on principle but on personality, and not by debate but by behind-the-scenes manipulation. The general picture of corruption and irresponsibility presented by the political parties was not an encouraging one, and it could hardly produce an atmosphere of firm conviction capable of standing up to bullying from the powerful services. As if the Chang Tso Lin episode had not been sufficient confirmation of this, warning cabinets of the dangers of vacillation, the army in Manchuria struck another blow in September 1931.

In what has since become a drearily familiar pattern in world politics, ambitious young officers, eager to overthrow constitutional government and to set up a separate state, decided to occupy Mukden and other major cities of Manchuria. In their view there was not much time. The ineffectiveness of Japanese cabinets in resisting the policy of the Chinese authorities in Manchuria (who were now trying to rid themselves of the Japanese economic stranglehold over mines and railways) would soon lead to the total loss of Japan's hard-won position. This time, the men on the spot – Kwantung Army officers – were not acting alone. They had full co-operation from friends in the General Staff HQ in Tokyo. The Foreign Office knew what was being planned through its consular officials in Manchuria, and Shidehara and his Prime Minister, Wakatsuki, prevailed upon the Emperor to rein in the army through its minister, General Minami. The Emperor agreed to do this and expressed his displeasure to Minami at the army's high-handed imperviousness to Tokyo decisions. Sensing the strength of the opposition, Minami complied with the Imperial request, but in a deliberately half-hearted way. He despatched Major-General Tatekawa to bear a letter to the Kwantung Army, ordering them to curb their appetite for creating incidents. Tatekawa was in no hurry. He did not take a plane but travelled by rail, and conveniently sent off a telegram announcing his journey and its purpose: to stop the outbreak of the incident planned by the Kwantung Army.

'Tatekawa expected arrive Mukden tomorrow hospitality requested.' It was carefully provided. Before Tatekawa delivered his important letter to the Commander-in-Chief, he was whisked away to a restaurant and there dined and wined into insensibility. At 10 o'clock that evening, while the party was still going strong, the South Manchurian Railway was ripped by explosions just north of Mukden. The anticipated fighting broke out between Chinese troops and Japanese Railway Guards. By next morning the Kwantung Army was in possession of Mukden. The road to the Pacific War was open.

Left: *Women cotton factory workers protest against low wages*

85

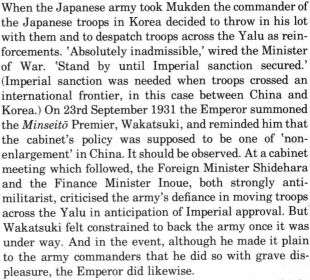

Chapter Six
The Thirties: Asian Expansion

When the Japanese army took Mukden the commander of the Japanese troops in Korea decided to throw in his lot with them and to despatch troops across the Yalu as reinforcements. 'Absolutely inadmissible,' wired the Minister of War. 'Stand by until Imperial sanction secured.' (Imperial sanction was needed when troops crossed an international frontier, in this case between China and Korea.) On 23rd September 1931 the Emperor summoned the *Minseitō* Premier, Wakatsuki, and reminded him that the cabinet's policy was supposed to be one of 'non-enlargement' in China. It should be observed. At a cabinet meeting which followed, the Foreign Minister Shidehara and the Finance Minister Inoue, both strongly anti-militarist, criticised the army's defiance in moving troops across the Yalu in anticipation of Imperial approval. But Wakatsuki felt constrained to back the army once it was under way. And in the event, although he made it plain to the army commanders that he did so with grave displeasure, the Emperor did likewise.

The political adventurism of the Kwantung Army highlighted the opposition between the army as a whole and the cabinet, in particular the Foreign Minister (and the Foreign Office, whose ambassadors abroad viewed with dismay the freedom with which the Wakatsuki cabinet appeared to permit the majors and colonels to go on the rampage).

A number of officers were involved later in 1931 in a plot known to history as 'The October Incident', which aimed at eliminating the cabinet altogether and replacing it by a military group. Once again those compromised were arrested. Once again they got away with negligible punishments at a time, it should be remembered, when the Peace Preservation Law was ensuring long terms of imprisonment for civilians engaged in left-wing political activities. Finally the Wakatsuki cabinet resigned, to make way for a *Seiyūkai* government under Inukai Tsuyoshi. Inukai was an odd mixture. His party was as

Left: Emperor Hirohito (on left) inspecting primitive, pre-radar sound-detectors for locating enemy aircraft, Osaka 1934

deeply committed to the interests of the Mitsui business combine as the *Minseitō* had been to Mitsubishi. But in his youth Inukai had been a colleague of Ōkuma Shigenobu and had resigned with him when Ōkuma courageously put forward in a very hostile climate a plea for constitutionalism and popular rights. Even though his party was committed to a strong line in China he had no sympathy at all for the usurpation of political power by the military.

But the army was no longer to be restrained. When fighting broke out in Shanghai between Chinese troops and a Japanese naval contingent stationed there, the army came to the navy's aid and put four divisions into the city before the fighting came to an end. Worse was to come. Under the aegis of the Kwantung Army the young heir of the vanished Manchu dynasty, Henry Pu Yi, was persuaded to mount the throne of the new state which the Japanese carved out of China. Manchukuo, as Manchuria was henceforth to be known, came into existence in March 1932. Faced with a fait accompli Inukai did his best and declared his intention of still recognising Chinese suzerainty over Manchuria, which should be governed by a separate regime; a totally independent state would bring Japan into conflict with the other signatories to the Nine-Power Treaty. Inukai thought his long political career had given him contacts in China his colleagues did not have. And he did not despair of reaching a modus vivendi with China. Underlining the importance of preserving the constitutional structure in Japan as a necessary preliminary to fruitful negotiation abroad, Inukai broadcast to the nation on 1st May 1932 denouncing extremists of both right and left and promising improvements in parliamentary government. A fortnight after this speech, on 15th May, a group of young army and navy officers broke into Inukai's house in broad daylight and assassinated him. The public, both at home and abroad, was profoundly shocked: at least, at the time. But when the assassins came up for trial enough time had elapsed for their view of themselves to be put across to public opinion in Japan, which began to side with them. It was believed that they had acted for patriotic reasons, and that the political parties and the industrial combines behind them were betraying Japan's true interests in Asia and at home. Inspired by the fascist ideas of Kita Ikki and the expansionist philosophy of Ōkawa Shūmei, the assassins were, no doubt, like many serving officers, deeply impressed by the suffering of the Japanese peas-

Left: The Japanese in Manchuria — soldier-settlers pay homage to their God-Emperor with the traditional banzai *(top); a meeting of the propagandist Manchukuan Concordia Society (bottom)*

antry – particularly in the north-east of Japan – in the years 1931 and 1932.

In the 1920s about 5,500,000 Japanese households engaged in agriculture cultivated plots of from 2 to 5 acres, with rice as the chief food crop, to which was devoted over half the cultivated area of the entire country. When rice prices were kept reasonably high, as in the late twenties, the farm households were fairly well off. But from 1927 onwards bumper crops succeeded one another, with an exceptionally large one in 1930. In spite of the government's attempts to keep prices steady by buying up surplus stocks, the price of rice began to plummet, and slid in four months in 1930-1 from 27 *yen* to 18 *yen* a *koku*. Japan's overseas expansion had exacted a price here, too: Korean rice production had risen by nearly a third in the twenty years following the annexation of 1910, and Formosa's rice harvests were richer than ever before. Japan had to import these harvests, because her growing population needed the extra rice. Consequently the Japanese farmer did not benefit from the population increase, which was met by cheaper rice from abroad.

There was the further complication of the American crash of 1929. Two-fifths of Japan's farming households had a secondary source of income, derived from the production of raw silk. By far the largest market for this silk was the USA. The unit of raw silk is the *kin*, which is roughly equal to $1\frac{1}{3}$ lbs. In 1923 100 *kin* were exported for 2,150 *yen*. From 1925 the price began to fall, but was still good compared to prices before the First World War. When the American market collapsed, the price per 100 *kin* swiftly fell to 540 *yen* by October 1930, and even as low as 390 *yen* by June 1932. Briefly, this meant that in terms of income from rice and silk the farmers' income had been cut in two – in some cases even by three-quarters. These statistics have to be seen in terms of the domestic tragedies they brought about. There was only one way open to farmers' daughters who were no longer able to work at raw silk production, and that was to work as prostitutes in the cities. Many households sold their daughters to procurers in order to stay alive. The *Minseitō* cabinet's relief measures were slow and inadequate, and the young officers whose recruits came from intolerably impoverished parts of Japan laid the blame for what happened at the door of Japan's party government and its big business connections. 'Peasant poverty,' writes a Japanese sociologist, 'was the direct cause of the Fascist movement becoming revolutionary and of the right-wing terrorism which broke out after 1931.'

Right: World depression struck Japan particularly hard. Acute poverty encouraged the search for revolutionary solutions

The soldiers intended to do far more than merely murder a prime minister. Power-stations, banks, and political party headquarters were attacked, and a situation was envisaged in which martial law would have to be imposed. From this it would only be a short step to military dictatorship. No wonder the Minister of War was hesitant in his condemnation: 'The crime was indeed committed in violation of national law, and therefore must be punished without mercy,' he proclaimed, 'but they acted neither for the sake of fame nor gain nor treason. They had no intention of committing treason. They acted upon the genuine belief that this was for the interest of the Imperial country. The case should not therefore be dealt with in a narrow-minded way.' It was not. One of the accomplices received a life sentence, the rest varying sentences down to four years. Eleven Military Academy students were sentenced by the army authorities to three months in prison.

Militarism rampant

The lesson of these sentences was not lost upon the army. When soundings were taken as to who should form a cabinet to succeed Inukai, it was learned that the army rejected any idea of a party cabinet. A coalition of *Seiyūkai* and *Minseitō* was formed under a former governor of Korea, Admiral Viscount Saitō, on 22nd May 1932, with General Araki Sadao as War Minister. It was thought, wrongly, that he could keep discipline among the younger officers. No doubt he could, but for his own purposes. Araki belonged to a faction in the army called the 'Imperial Way School' *(Kōdō-ha)* which exerted a good deal of influence until the mid-thirties, when a rival faction, the 'Control School' *(Tōsei-ha),* began to play the dominant role. Neither faction had any sympathy for constitutional forms of government and in effect Inukai's cabinet proved to be the last party cabinet Japan was to know until the end of the Second World War. But there *were* differences. The *Tōsei-ha* was more concerned with exploiting China as an end in itself than was the *Kōdō-ha*, whose members were obsessed by the fear of Soviet Communism and regarded it as a certainty that one day Japan and Russia would be at war.

Meanwhile there was the League of Nations to be faced. A commission of the League, headed by Lord Lytton, had carried out an investigation into the Manchurian Incident and the setting up of Manchukuo. Its report came out in October 1932 and made it plain that the Manchurian regime had not been called into being by a genuine and spontaneous independence movement. While conceding that Japan's share in the economic development of Manchuria should be safeguarded, it also de-

clared that armed forces should be withdrawn. Japan's action in recognising Manchukuo as an independent state in September 1932 was a deliberate flouting of China's sovereignty, and a fateful concession to the Kwantung Army and its sympathisers. In spite of the wishes of the Prime Minister, indeed of the Emperor himself, the Japanese government determined to ignore the Lytton Report, and its delegates walked out of the League of Nations meeting in Geneva in February 1933. The Army had successfully dictated the course of Japan's foreign policy. It was now to turn to home affairs.

'The Army', of course, is a blanket term: it makes the reality seem unified and consistent. It was not. Although most sections of army opinion shared a contempt for party politics and desired Japanese expansion in Asia, the army was deeply divided in itself. The internal struggle for power between the *Kōdō-ha* and the *Tōsei-ha* was fought out in Manchuria and in Tokyo itself. On the morning of 26th February 1936 the *Kōdō-ha* made its crucial bid for power. Captains and lieutenants of the First Division, at the head of about 1,500 men, marched through the snow in the streets of the capital to take over the central buildings of government; the Diet, the War Ministry, the Metropolitan Police Office, the Prime Minister's residence, all were occupied. It was the 15th May (1932) episode all over again, but on a larger scale. Squads of soldiers were sent to hunt down Prime Minister Okada, the Minister of Finance, the Emperor's chief adviser Count Makino and several other government functionaries. The assassins did not know what the Prime Minister looked like and murdered his brother-in-law by mistake. Although they kept watch on the house the Prime Minister, dressed as a mourner, managed to escape by following his brother-in-law's coffin. Makino and Suzuki, an Imperial Grand Chamberlain, had narrow escapes. The others, very old men, were savagely butchered under the eyes of their families.

Then the rebels came to a halt. For four days they continued to occupy the centre of Tokyo, expecting their seniors in the War Office to declare for them. Closely guarded in the Military Club, the War Minister and members of the Supreme Military Council attempted to negotiate. The young officers addressed curious knots of passers-by and issued a Manifesto laying the blame for unrest in the army and for the strained relations between Japan and the rest of the world on the shoulders of the elder statesmen, the business magnates, the bureaucracy, and the political parties. 'Therefore,' they concluded with blood-chilling candour, 'it is our duty as subjects of

Left: Japanese soldiers bear the ashes of fallen comrades

His Majesty the Emperor to safeguard our country by killing those responsible . . .'

His Majesty the Emperor was in no doubt about the quality of their actions. When the Press with habitual euphemism referred to 'the incident' or 'the affair', the Emperor bluntly told the War Minister: 'This is mutiny.' An appeal to surrender, signed by the Tokyo garrison commander and referring to the Emperor's wish that the soldiers return to their barracks, was dropped on the insurgents from the air. It was finally heeded. One of the captains shot himself. Possibly anticipating a trial by court-martial which would give them a chance to propagate their case by public statements printed in the Press, the others did nothing. Fifteen of them were tried by secret court-martial and shot in a Tokyo military prison. Some of their civilian mentors, among them Kita Ikki, were executed the following year.

From the point of view of the Army's internal political structure, the collapse of the insurgents was the collapse of a segment of field-rank opinion (though a number of generals, like Araki and Mazaki, were involved) linked with the fascist theories of Kita Ikki and the populist radicalism stemming from agrarian unrest. It was a clear victory for the senior generals of the *Tōsei-ha* (Umezu, Koiso, Sugiyama, Tōjō) who in future could always point to the possible recurrence of violent insubordination as a means of obtaining what they wanted. This was shown almost at once in the selection of the Hirota cabinet which succeeded Okada. Yoshida Shigeru, who had the reputation of being a liberal and was later to be the best-known and most-admired prime minister of the post-1945 era, was proposed as Foreign Minister. A liberal Tokyo University professor, Mikami, was proposed as Minister of Education. The War Minister, Terauchi, successfully vetoed both proposals.

Abroad, Japan was becoming increasingly involved both politically and militarily with north China and, on the political level, with the European powers whose authoritarian structure was more sympathetic to her own than that of the democratic regimes of England, France, and the USA. In November 1936 she became a signatory to the Anti-Comintern Pact, an alliance with Germany directed against Soviet Russia and containing a secret annexe by which, if Russia attacked any of the signatories, they would meet at once to discuss the defence of their common interests. Japan was showing some signs of economic recovery from the distress of the early thirties, but many army officers still chafed at being held

Right: Pilots of the Japanese Air Force pledge the success of their mission over China *(top)*; the cruiser Ashigara *(bottom)*

on the leash in China. As they saw it, tariff barriers raised by European nations and by the USA were making trade difficult for Japan, whose population had increased by 5,000,000 between 1930 and 1935. Immigration was no answer to this, since the very countries which raised tariff barriers were also those whose racialist policies limited Japanese emigration. The only outlet remaining was expansion on the Asian mainland, with the army paving the way.

The 'China Incident'

No one was very surprised, then, when news came from China that fighting had broken out—yet again—near Peking on the night of 7th July 1937. An infantry company, on night manoeuvres near Lukouchiao (the Marco Polo Bridge) in the suburbs of Peking, had exchanged shots with elements of the Chinese 29th Army stationed in the walled town of Wanping. When the Japanese insisted on being admitted to the town to find the Chinese said to be responsible for opening fire, the garrison refused them entry. The Japanese brought up artillery, and the fighting gradually spread to Peking and Tientsin, which were occupied by early August. The 'China Incident' had begun. The Minister of War, General Sugiyama, who belonged to the *Tōsei-ha,* promptly asked the cabinet to authorise reinforcements. Soon 150,000 Japanese troops were engaged in hostilities, which were still called by the euphemism 'incident'. The Japanese moved out of north China into the great cities of the south, first Shanghai, then Nanking, where terrible massacres of the inhabitants took place. The League of Nations condemned Japan's violation of the Nine-Power Treaty, but Japan contemptuously refused to attend a conference convened in Brussels to discuss putting an end to the fighting. The Japanese army was not going to be stopped so easily. It moved on up the Yangtze from Nanking, shelling a British Navy gunboat, while Japanese navy bombers sank the USS *Panay*. The troops in north China and those operating in the Yangtze valley joined forces in 1938. In October of that year Hankow was taken, and then Canton.

For a moment it seemed as if the impression created by the horrifying atrocities in Nanking, and then by the sinking of the *Panay,* might bring the USA to China's aid. But isolationism was still too strong, and the Japanese government was quick to apologise. That Japanese public opinion was by no means universally behind what her military were doing was shown quite clearly by the numbers of ordinary Japanese from all walks of life who called at the American Embassy or wrote to Ambassador Grew to express their shame and regrets for the

action of their navy. 'One well-dressed Japanese woman,' Grew noted in his diary for 20th December 1937, 'stepped behind a door in the chancery and cut off a big strand of her hair and gave it to us with a carnation — the old-fashioned gesture of mourning for the loss of a husband. Another Japanese broke down and cried at his country's shame.'

From the army's point of view their successes were the final justification of their policies over the previous decade. At last, in a matter of months, they had penetrated in force to the heart of China. By November 1938 they controlled nearly all China's richest and most populous provinces and most of her coastline. Chiang Kai-shek had retreated to Chungking, far to the west, and must surely negotiate and surrender soon. In any case the Japanese knew there was a minority in Chiang's own cabinet which was willing to make peace. Protests from the Western powers could be dismissed as the hypocrisy of those who saw their own loot being removed from under their very noses. Had they hesitated to use their commerce to plunder China and back it up by military force when they thought fit? By what right did they criticise Japan when she fulfilled her natural destiny in the same way? Japan was carrying out something very similar to what was emerging in Europe: the establishment of a New Order.

The Prime Minister, Prince Konoye Fumimaro, a member of a very old aristocratic family, who had taken office with some reluctance in June 1937, felt incapable of resisting the demands of the military. 'We are their puppets,' he had said of his government on one occasion, and it is perhaps an indication of the desperate situation in which he found himself that Konoye's only answer was to back *Kōdō-ha* elements in the army to balance the now ungovernable *Tōsei-ha* and, failing this, to resign, which he did in January 1939.

Left: Japanese victory march through Shanghai, December 1937

The Spread of Extremism

The 1930s have often been termed by the Japanese *kurai tanima,* the 'dark valley'. This was the decade when military fascism ran riot, expressing itself in unchecked aggression abroad and murderous violence at home. There was much talk in military circles of a 'Shōwa Restoration', whereby the monster capitalist concerns, the *zaibatsu,* would be forced to give up their riches, and the political parties would yield their powers to the Emperor and the armed forces. A rash of military coups and assassinations followed, while the army itself was faction-torn. Though the Emperor was constitutionally the sovereign power and personally more farsighted than most, it is doubtful whether even he could have reversed events. Here he is shown taking a military review **(top right)**. As early as 1934 women underwent military training **(bottom right)**. Final proof that the old *samurai* code was dead is illustrated by the new-fangled Japanese habit of using dead Chinese for bayonet practice **(below)**

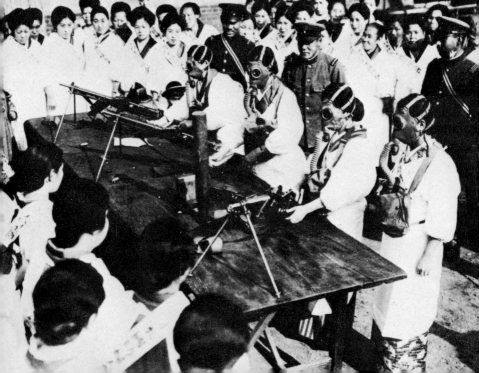

Chapter 7
War in the Pacific

By the time Konoye resigned it was obvious that the European powers were likely to be wrapped up in their own affairs for some time to come. The outbreak of war in Europe in September 1939 was eight months away, and it seemed that whatever aim Hitler set himself he could achieve, either by the use of force or through the pusillanimity of the victors of 1918. It was a pattern the Japanese militarists easily recognised. They had successfully broken up party government in the Diet, now little more than a trivial debating chamber which exercised almost no control over the cabinet at all, which was formed without regard to the strength of parties. They had instituted witch-hunts against those Liberal thinkers who had analysed Japan's history and social structure in terms different from those found in the school text-book mythology. Japan's foremost constitutional lawyer, Professor Minobe Tatsukichi, who was also a member of the House of Peers, had taught consistently, since 1911, that the Emperor of Japan was an organ of the state: a theory which followed naturally, he said, from Prince Itō's definition of the Emperor as 'head' of state, and one which had been freely accepted by Japan's constitutional lawyers. General Baron Kikuchi denounced Minobe's book in which this theory was put forward, in the House of Peers in February 1934. 'Merely to think of our Emperor as the same as the Chinese Emperor or any Western sovereign,' he complained, 'is to forfeit the secret of our national policy. If we do not stamp out the thought of scholars and politicians who hold these views, the future of our nation will be threatened.' A year later he returned to the attack, quite unappeased by Minobe's carefully reasoned justification of his case, and in April 1935 the Home Ministry banned Minobe's writings. Minobe himself had to resign from the House of Peers and was threatened with proceedings for lèse-majesté. He was even assaulted and wounded by a fanatic in February 1936.

A government prepared to allow the hounding of a man

Left: An Italian postcard lauds Japan's victories in the Pacific

of Minobe's standing and calibre was clearly ripe for an alliance with the book-burners of Nazi Germany, and the army worked hard towards this end, particularly through Japan's very pro-Nazi envoy in Berlin, General Ōshima. Baron Hiranuma succeeded Konoye in 1939, and his cabinet met seventy times, to no avail, in deliberations upon the possibilities of such an alliance. Although the army wanted it, the navy and the Foreign Office did not. Hiranuma's government was not averse to a German pact directed against Soviet Russia, but it did not wish to be drawn into war with Great Britain and France if and whenever Germany chose to attack her. By the end of May 1939, after countless telegrams had passed between Berlin and Tokyo, no agreement had been reached, and on 22nd May Germany and Italy signed a bilateral pact. The Japanese attitude, Hitler complained in exasperation to Ribbentrop, was becoming less and less comprehensible.

The feeling was mutual, as was shown four months later when Germany signed a non-aggression pact with the Soviet Union. The Japanese appear to have had no wind of this, and Hiranuma resigned, declaring he could not cope with a diplomatic situation as baffling as that in Eastern Europe. Japanese troops had already tangled with the Red Army on the frontiers of Manchuria in the Changkufeng episode of July 1938 and the Nomonhan incident of May 1939, which dragged on and on until September with the Japanese incurring heavy casualties, at the very time Germany and Russia were celebrating their newly-discovered agreement. A soldier and a sailor – General Abe and Admiral Yonai – followed Hiranuma at the head of Japan's government in the crucial year that led from the British declaration of war in September 1939 to Germany's triumph in the summer of 1940. Anti-British and anti-American feelings were running high in Japan by this time; the Japanese deliberately set out to humiliate British subjects in Tientsin in the summer of 1939 and blockaded the French and British concessions. Then the temporary eclipse of France in June 1940 turned Japan's eyes southward, and made a new purpose possible.

To put an end to the 'China Incident' when by all military rules it should already be over, Japan began to put pressure on those peripheral countries through which Chiang Kai-shek was being supplied and kept going. In February 1939 Hainan Island, off the south China coast, had been occupied, which was an obvious move in the

Right: *The 1938 Empire Day procession winds through the streets of Tokyo after visiting the Yasukuni Shrine.* **Far right:** *A French cartoon of 1934 prophesies the future* **(top)**; *Matsuoka, the Japanese Foreign Minister, talks with Hitler* **(bottom)**

102

direction of French Indo-China. Supplies had been passing through Haiphong harbour, up through Tonkin, and into Yunnan, just as they had been going up the Burma Road from Rangoon via Lashio to Kunming, China's back door. Japan succeeded in March 1940 in setting up a puppet regime under Chiang Kai-shek's colleague, Wang Ching Wei, who established his government in Nanking. He was easily the most important Asian politician to declare for the 'New Order in East Asia' until Subhas Chandra Bose put himself at the head of the Indian National Army on the side of Japan in 1943. But neither political nor military pressure in China brought about the long-desired result.

On 19th June 1940 Japan's Foreign Minister insisted that the French government allow Japanese inspectors to investigate arms shipments passing to Chiang Kai-shek through northern Indo-China. Japanese troops in the Chinese province of Kwangsi moved up to the Indo-Chinese border, and Japanese naval vessels made a show of strength off Haiphong. The French colony, under its governor-general, Catroux, was on its own. Metropolitan France could not send aid, the British had none to give, the Americans expressed regret, Catroux had almost no air power, and he estimated that his 50,000 troops had about enough supplies to last for a month. He bowed to the inevitable and, hoping by partial appeasement to keep large Japanese forces out of French Indo-China, he closed the railway to Yunnan on 16th July 1940. His successor, Admiral Decoux, tried to fend off further Japanese pressure by insisting that Tokyo treat direct with Paris where, he may have hoped, Marshal Pétain might conceivably induce the Germans to defend French interests in the East. It was a waste of time. On 2nd August 1940 Tokyo sent another ultimatum, direct to Decoux, demanding transit rights for Japanese troops across Tonkin and the use of airfields. On 30th August Japan and France devised a formula whereby Japan recognised French sovereignty over Indo-China in return for economic agreements and military facilities. Three weeks later, Decoux surrendered to further demands after a brisk exchange with the Japanese from Kwangsi had shown that his local forces under French officers were no match for the China-hardened Japanese. Soon several thousand Japanese troops were quartered in Tonkin.

Japan then turned to diplomatic pressure. She had already successfully compelled Great Britain to close the Burma Road supply route to China on 18th August 1940 (it was re-opened on 18th October). Then hostilities broke out between France and Siam—the latter un-

Left: Graduation ceremonies for pilots promoted self-sacrifice

doubtedly egged on by the Japanese to regain what it regarded as its lost provinces, Laotian territory on the right bank of the Mekong, ceded to France in 1904. After a number of indecisive encounters the French were beaten on land and soundly thrashed the Siamese at sea. The Japanese stepped in to mediate, awarding rich rice-growing Cambodian territory to Siam in the peace treaty which was signed in Tokyo on 9th May 1941. By this act Japan had established herself as the arbiter of destiny in South-East Asia, and as the price of her unwanted mediation obtained the right to station troops in southern Indo-China as well as the north. They landed in Saigon on 28th July 1941, their chief-of-staff being Chō Isamu, a firebrand from the days of the October Incident 1931. The Japanese Foreign Minister, Admiral Toyoda, explained to the American ambassador Grew that Japan would withdraw from Indo-China once the China Incident was closed; but the Americans were sceptical. It was obvious enough, Roosevelt said, that Japan was in Indo-China 'for the purpose of further offence'.

Matsuoka's plans for the New East Asian Order

The decisions of the European powers had influenced Japan. In July 1940 Prince Konoye had returned to power once again, with the brilliant and aggressive Matsuoka Yōsuke as his Foreign Minister. 'A dynamic and erratic genius,' writes a Japanese Foreign Ministry official of him; 'a talkative chauvinist' is the view of a recent English historian. Matsuoka had no doubt that Germany would soon control Europe for a long time to come, and this would provide Japan with the opportunity to move south and obtain the rich resources of raw materials in the colonies of the defeated powers, tin and rubber from Malaya, rice from Indo-China, oil from the Netherlands East Indies. Matsuoka finally persuaded the cabinet to sign the Tripartite Pact with Germany and Italy on 27th September 1940. The aim was by this time quite different from what it had been when first envisaged. When the Germans first proposed such a pact in 1938, the ultimate target was Soviet Russia which had now, since August 1939, been on 'friendly' terms with Germany. So when the Pact was finally signed, it became clear that its target was Great Britain and her overseas

Right: The headstrong Foreign Minister, Matsuoka Yōsuke.
Top right: The Time cover of 22nd December 1941, referring to Pearl Harbor, featured 'Japan's Aggressor: Admiral Yamamoto'.
Bottom right: Evidence of Japan's New Asian Order: a propaganda leaflet depicts an Indian accusing his countrymen for enduring the 'rule of blood by the whites'. The skulls symbolise the Indian Mutiny and the Indian dead of the First World War

empire. Article II of the Pact read: 'Germany and Italy shall recognise and respect the leadership of Japan in the establishment of a new order in East Asia.' To the Japanese this implied recognition by an important segment of European opinion of Japan's ancient ideal of *Hakkō ichiu* ('the eight corners of the world under one roof') – a universal brotherhood under the overall aegis of the Japanese Imperial House. That this was a definite scheme for a large portion of the earth's surface, and not mere windy rhetoric, was shown by plans drawn up by the Ministry of War in December 1941: some East Asian countries (Burma and Malaya for instance) would have monarchies of their own; Pacific and Indian Ocean territories of the USA and the European colonial powers would be reconstituted as governments-general of the Japanese Empire – Ceylon, Australia, New Zealand, Alaska, the Yukon, Alberta, British Columbia, the State of Washington, the Central American Republics, the British, Dutch, and French West Indies. The colonies of the European powers would be taken first, in one war; then there would be a pause of twenty years, and a final war after which the second group would be taken.

Matsuoka's attempted diplomatic realignment fitted this scheme. He had determined to turn the Tripartite Pact ultimately into a four-power agreement, to include Soviet Russia, so guaranteeing Japan's northern frontiers in Manchuria. In the pursuit of this aim Matsuoka visited Europe and, after spending nearly an hour in Moscow lecturing Stalin on Japan's ideology, signed a neutrality pact with Russia in April 1941 – 'a historic reversal in Japanese-Soviet relations', as *Izvestia* called it. His colleagues in the cabinet nonetheless thought Matsuoka's diplomacy, effective though it was, risked bringing Japan into war with the USA before she achieved her aims in South-East Asia. Two missions had already been sent to the Netherlands East Indies to negotiate an economic agreement – the Kobayashi Mission in October 1940 and the Yoshizawa Mission, January-June 1941. On 14th May the Japanese delegation presented proposals which would have meant 75-100 per cent of Netherlands East Indies exports going to Japan, the crucial item being a request to the government to ensure that oil companies operating there stepped exports to Japan up to 3,800,000 tons per annum. The Netherlands delegation presented their answer on 6th June 1941, making minor concessions but pointing out that the increase of oil exports remained a matter to be decided between the oil companies and Japanese importers, the reserves situation not permitting, in their view, an increase in production. On 17th June the Japanese delegation saw the governor-general and declared

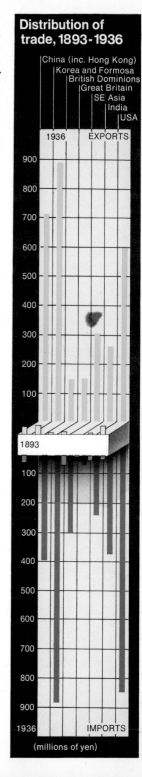

Distribution of trade, 1893-1936

China (inc. Hong Kong)
Korea and Formosa
British Dominions
Great Britain
SE Asia
India
USA

1936　　EXPORTS

900
800
700
600
500
400
300
200
100

1893

100
200
300
400
500
600
700
800
900

1936　　IMPORTS

(millions of yen)

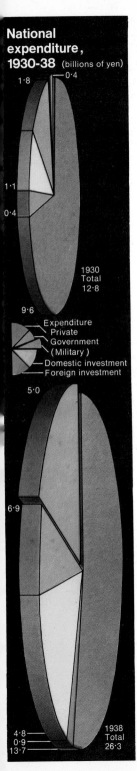

National expenditure, 1930-38 (billions of yen)

1·8
0·4

1·1

0·4

1930
Total
12·8

9·6

Expenditure
Private
Government
(Military)
Domestic investment
Foreign investment

5·0

6·9

1938
Total
26·3

4·8
0·9
13·7

the negotiations had been unsuccessful, to the accompaniment of an angry chorus from the Japanese press. But the importance of the news was overshadowed within the week when Hitler invaded Russia, a development which seems to have taken Konoye and Matsuoka unawares, though their ambassador in Berlin, Ōshima, had told them what was going to happen two weeks before it did.

This put them in a quandary. The Soviet Union, through Hitler's action, now stood in the democratic camp; but this fact in itself would not decide how Japan should move. Her northern frontiers were previously secured by agreement. Now they were secured by Russia's fight to the death with Germany. Japan might conceivably attack across the Manchurian border, with the possibility of making some gains in Siberia as the prize. Or she could use the free hand given her by Russia's preoccupation elsewhere to move south, and, in doing so, finish the China Incident at one and the same time. The difficulty was the increasingly antagonistic attitude of the USA.

America turns hostile

American opinion, which had grown increasingly suspicious of Japanese aims, at any rate since the beginning of the China Incident, was now almost uniformly hostile. In the 1920s some American officials in China had felt that the presence of Japanese troops was a comforting one for business interests, and as late as November 1937 Ambassador Grew hoped that his countrymen would not accept the view 'that Japan has been a big bully and China the downtrodden victim'. America had later tried to keep out of actual political involvement, so long as her economic interest and her 'long-established rights in China' were safeguarded. When it became clear that this particular status quo would not survive Japanese occupation of the whole of China, the USA's attitude hardened. When a new commercial treaty between Japan and the USA was proposed in 1939, Cordell Hull, the American Secretary of State, refused to negotiate 'unless Japan completely changed her attitude and practice towards our rights and interests in China'. A few months later, in July 1940, an embargo was placed on aviation fuel – a crucial munition of war – followed in September by an embargo on scrap iron, then in November by another on exports of iron and steel. But none of these measures hit Japan as hard as the freezing of Japanese assets in **112** ▷

Left: Trade and expenditure diagrams for Japan pre-1939. They show that any economic embargo on Japan would leave her with little choice other than war. Both Great Britain and America underrated Japan's war potential. They believed that economic sanctions would compel her evacuation of China

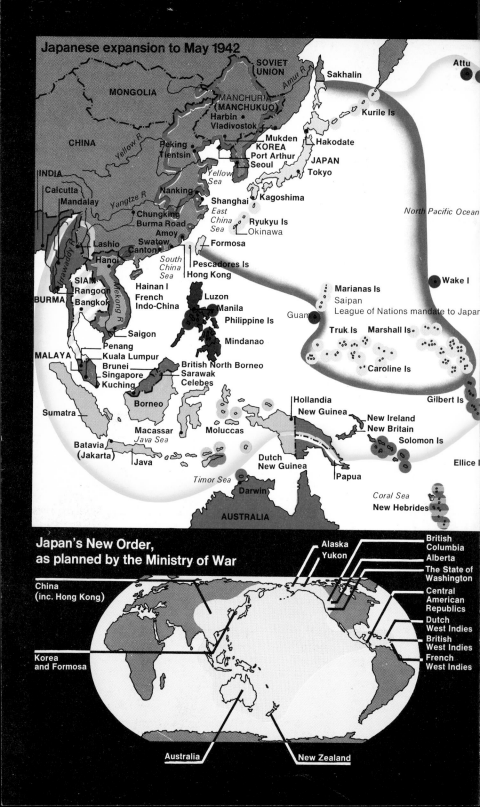

Japanese expansion to May 1942

SOVIET UNION
MONGOLIA
MANCHURIA (MANCHUKUO)
Harbin
Vladivostok
CHINA
Peking
Tientsin
Mukden
KOREA
Port Arthur
Seoul
Hakodate
JAPAN
Tokyo
INDIA
Calcutta
Mandalay
Nanking
Yellow Sea
Kagoshima
Chungking
Shanghai
Burma Road
East China Sea
Amoy
Ryukyu Is
Lashio
Swatow
Okinawa
Hanoi
Canton
Formosa
South China Sea
SIAM
Pescadores Is
Hainan I
Hong Kong
Rangoon
French
BURMA
Bangkok
Indo-China
Luzon
Saigon
Manila
Penang
Philippine Is
MALAYA
Kuala Lumpur
Mindanao
Brunei
British North Borneo
Singapore
Sarawak
Kuching
Celebes
Sumatra
Borneo
Hollandia
New Guinea
Macassar
Moluccas
Java Sea
Batavia (Jakarta)
Java
Dutch New Guinea
Papua
Timor Sea
Darwin
AUSTRALIA

Sakhalin
Attu
Kurile Is
North Pacific Ocean
Wake I
Marianas Is
Saipan
League of Nations mandate to Japan
Guam
Truk Is
Marshall Is
Caroline Is
Gilbert Is
New Ireland
New Britain
Solomon Is
Ellice I
Coral Sea
New Hebrides

Japan's New Order, as planned by the Ministry of War

China (inc. Hong Kong)

Korea and Formosa

Alaska
Yukon

British Columbia
Alberta
The State of Washington
Central American Republics
Dutch West Indies
British West Indies
French West Indies

Australia

New Zealand

The New Order in East Asia

Bering
Sea   ALASKA

Dutch Harbour
Aleutian Is

Midway

Pearl Harbor
Hawaiian Is
    Hawaii

Johnston I

South Pacific Ocean

200 400 600 ML
  400   800 KM

● Japanese
● Allied to Japan
■ Japanese expansion
  to July 1941
■ Japanese expansion
  to May 1942
● Dutch
  American
  Portuguese
  British
  British
  Commonwealth
● Australian
● French

Japan's war aim, expressed in her propaganda as the protection of East Asia from Anglo-American exploitation, was to secure her own acceptance as the 'light of Asia' — the political leader of all the Asiatic peoples within the Greater East Asian Co-prosperity Sphere (**bottom**, opposite). Economic self-sufficiency lay at the root of Japan's expansionist plans. Once the rich resources of tin, rubber, and oil belonging to Malaya and the Netherlands East Indies had fallen to Japan in 1942 (**top**, opposite), Prime Minister Tōjō (**below**) declared that Japan was no longer a 'have-not' nation. Her past record lent little credibility to her promises of future independence, and countries like Burma and the Philippines soon found that freedom came a long way second to co-operation with Japan. Yet the Pan-Asiatic note she struck and the anti-European sentiments she whipped up ensured effectively that — whatever the outcome of the war — the old colonial order would never return.

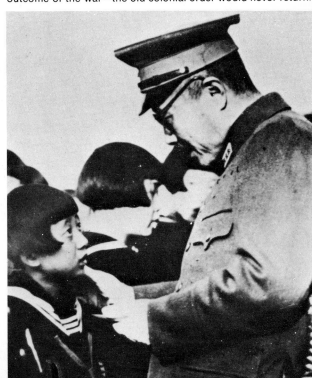

the USA on 25th July 1941. The USA carried out this measure, it declared, at the express wish of Chiang Kai-shek. It was not, therefore, a direct answer to events in French Indo-China but had the effect of seeming to be so, since on 26th July Japan made public its plan to occupy strategic areas in the south of Indo-China, and began unloading her troops in the docks of Saigon two days later. On 1st August the final step of imposing an oil embargo was taken by the USA. Now Japan could trade only with Manchuria, China, Thailand, and French Indo-China.

The asset freeze hit Japan hard. Her government expenditure had risen by nearly 50 per cent during the thirties, most of it on the army and navy. Her heavy industries had expanded and re-equipped, but her farmers, overloaded with debts and taxation, suffered heavily from the world financial depression and there was a drift to the towns, where 1,000,000 new factory jobs were available between 1930 and 1936 (a quarter of Japan's workers were in mining or the constructional and manufacturing industries). This leap forward in industrialisation had made her a market for raw materials, and by 1936 half of the USA's exports to Asia went to Japan alone. In 1938 Japan owned a third of the world's merchant shipping tonnage—freight dues paid for one-tenth of her exports. These themselves were part of a shifting picture: the old currency-earning staple, raw silk, had fallen to 14 per cent of the total by 1938, and heavy industry (metals, chemicals, engineering) was assuming a major role. This meant she was fully enmeshed in the web of international trade relations and needed overseas supplies as never before in her history: one-fifth of her rice and beans came from overseas, one-third of her fats and oils, four-fifths of her iron and steel, and all her wool, rubber, and raw cotton (she was by now the world's chief exporter of cotton piece goods). One-fifth of her economy, by 1940, was working for war. That economy the USA now deliberately attempted to strangle.

Last-minute peace manoeuvres
At the same time as the USA was escalating economic reprisals on Japan in an attempt to restrain her from further military adventures in Asia, peace moves were being tested at various levels. Secret talks took place between Roosevelt's Postmaster-General, Walker, and two Catholic missionaries who acted as go-betweens for Japanese military and business interests. Secretary of State Hull, who disapproved strongly of these semi-official approaches, and the Japanese ambassador, an old navy man, Admiral Nomura, had been meeting on and off since February 1941. In these exchanges the Americans, like the British, had the upper hand because they

had broken the Japanese diplomatic code and read every telegram that passed between Tokyo and Washington. It is, incidentally, this element of foreknowledge which in the minds of certain historians has built up a case against American policy in 1941. This policy, they claim, constituted a deliberate attempt, in the light of full awareness of Japan's intentions, to goad Japan into a situation from which she had no alternative other than to strike back.

At the very highest level of all Prince Konoye wondered whether a person-to-person discussion between himself and Roosevelt might provide the ultimate dramatic denouement to all the mounting crises. Could peace suddenly be produced by direct confrontation? He got rid of the aggressive, too-dynamic Matsuoka in July 1941 by the roundabout way of dissolving his cabinet and then reconstructing its successor without him. On 6th September 1941 he and Grew dined together at the house of a mutual friend. Konoye told Grew that he, Konoye, bore the responsibility for the deterioration in relations between Japan and the USA. He was also, therefore, the one who should improve them. He accepted Hull's four principles as a beginning:

 i respect for the sovereignty and territorial integrity of all nations
 ii non-interference in other countries' internal affairs
 iii equality of commercial opportunity
 iv non-disturbance of the Pacific status quo, other than by peaceful change.

He would like to meet Roosevelt, he said, 'with the least possible delay', and was prepared to go to Honolulu or Alaska to do this. Roosevelt did not accept the invitation, on the grounds that nothing would be achieved so long as negotiations at ambassadorial level had proved futile; and also perhaps because he believed Konoye could not take the rest of Japan with him, particularly the military, if he *did* agree to a settlement with the USA. He may well have been right, because the service chiefs gave Konoye clearly to understand that they had no intention of withdrawing from China — an indispensable preliminary to having America's oil embargo lifted — and that they now regarded South-East Asia as the next objective.

An Imperial Conference had taken place earlier on the same day in the Emperor's presence, at which the decision was made to be prepared for war by the end of October 1941 even if this involved the USA; to exhaust all possible diplomatic means, at the same time, to reach an agreement with the USA and Great Britain; and if negotiations for an amicable settlement proved fruitless

Left: Japanese troops continuing their advance in North China

by the beginning of October, Japan should determine on war with the USA, Great Britain, and the Netherlands.

It was normally the Emperor's practice to preside in silence over such conferences. Unexpectedly he broke into this one. The high command, he believed, had not given a clear answer to a question put by Baron Hara, the President of the Privy Council. Did the decisions imply that precedence was given to diplomacy or war? General Sugiyama and Admiral Nagano, army and navy chiefs-of-staff, sat silent. 'The high command, to our deep regret,' said the Emperor, 'has not seen fit to clarify this question.' He then took a piece of paper from his pocket, saying, 'Our august ancestor, the Emperor Meiji, once wrote a poem. We will read it to you now:

> In this world we are all brothers
> Yet there is constant trouble and no peace.
> Why should this be?'

His grandfather's ideal of peace, he said, was his own. His questioning of Sugiyama's ability to make war successfully in the Pacific showed where his doubts lay. 'When you were Minister of War,' he said, 'you predicted Chiang Kai-shek would be quickly defeated. It hasn't happened yet.' If Sugiyama could not conclude the China Incident, what guarantee was there that the upshot of an adventure into the vastness of the Pacific would produce more immediate results?

The service chiefs expressed their fear of causing the Emperor displeasure. But they returned from the conference to their war games. Plan Z—the attack on Pearl Harbor—was debated in the Naval War College and adopted in October. Operations in the Pacific and South-East Asia were rehearsed between 1st and 5th October at the Army War College. Then active preparations for the campaigns began. The southern operations would take five months, requiring at least 400,000 tons of merchant shipping. 4,000,000 men would ultimately be deployed. The sooner hostilities began the better, the high command thought. Oil for civilian stocks would be exhausted by the middle of 1942, paralysing the country's main industries. The navy had two years' supply for its fleet and air forces.

In desperation Konoye asked Bishop Walsh (the missionary who had already negotiated through Walker for him in Washington) to tell Roosevelt that if no serious American proposal were received soon he would be unable to hold his position any longer. Time was running out for him in any case. Before Walsh had a chance to reach the USA Konoye's cabinet resigned under pressure from its War Minister, General Tōjō Hideki. On 16th October

Right: *Pearl Harbor—the American Pacific Fleet lies crippled*

114

1941 the Emperor summoned Tōjō to take over the government, and instructed him specifically to obtain collaboration between army and navy (Tōjō had already expressed the fear that the navy was about to rat and leave the burden of the decision to the army); and he was to disregard the 6th September Conference decision and reshape national policy – in effect, either to bring negotiations with America to a satisfactory conclusion, or lead Japan into war.

The American ambassador in the teeth of the evidence refused to believe that Japan was necessarily moving closer to a military dictatorship. In fact, he thought, Tōjō might well be able to restrain the army where Konoye had failed. Because Tōjō was a full general on active service, 'the Japanese army for the first time in recent years,' wrote Grew, 'has openly assumed responsibility for the policies and conduct of Japan, which it had previously steadfastly declined to accept.' It would be logical to expect that General Tōjō would be in a position to control extremist groups. At a conference between the government and the high command which took place from 23rd October to 2nd November 1941, the American Bureau of the Foreign Office, which contained many men who had been educated in the USA, made a detailed case against Japan throwing in her lot irrevocably with the Axis powers: Japan should stay neutral and solve the China Incident by negotiation. These pleas went unheeded and the conference broke up, with the familiar decision to pursue negotiations while at the same time preparing for the worst.

On 28th November 1941 the Japanese government received a set of American proposals, the so-called 'Hull Note'. Its terms were these:

  i Japan should withdraw all military, air, and police forces from China and Indo-China

  ii Japan should withdraw all support for any regime in China other than Chiang Kai-shek's

  iii Japan should nullify the pact with Germany and Italy

  iv Japan should sign a non-aggression pact with the USA, Great Britain, China, the Netherlands, the Soviet Union, and Thailand.

It was, the Japanese felt, as if the negotiations had never even begun. The Americans would not have sent a note which played so obviously into the hands of Japan's military extremists if they had not already determined on war. The British ambassador, Sir Robert Craigie, did not know about the Hull Note until months after the war had broken out. He then expressed to Kase Toshikazu, a Japanese Foreign Ministry official, his regret that Great Britain had at Churchill's express wish left negotiations

with Japan to the Americans. Anybody who understood the mentality of the Japanese people, he told Kase, would have known that such proposals at such a time would deeply wound their susceptibilities and possibly cause negotiations to break down.

Two attempts were made to halt the juggernaut. On 29th November 1941 the Emperor convened a meeting at the Imperial Palace of eight *jūshin* (senior statesmen who had held the office of Premier) – Abe, Hayashi, Hiranuma, Hirota, Konoye, Okada, Wakatsuki, Yonai, together with the new President of the Privy Council, Baron Hara. Tōjō and his new Foreign Minister, Tōgō Shigenori, analysed the situation for them in a morning-long session. They then lunched with the Emperor and afterwards gave him their views individually. Most of them wanted peace and recommended moderation. Wakatsuki did not believe Japan could stand a long war, nor did Okada, because of inadequate war materials. Konoye admitted negotiations had collapsed but did not think rushing into war was the only alternative; why not play for time? Yonai and Hirota concurred. But Hiranuma and the two army generals, Abe and Hayashi, declared that war was the only course left open. The following day, the Emperor's younger brother, Prince Takamatsu, who happened also to be a naval officer, told him the navy was not ready for war. The Navy Minister and Chief-of-Staff contradicted this: as they were bound to, since they knew a naval force had already set sail, four days before, from Hitokappu in the Kurile Islands eastwards into the Pacific. The decision to make war was finally taken at an Imperial Conference on 1st December 1941.

The Pacific War unfolds
The first campaigns amply justified the confidence of Japan's service chiefs. Aircraft from the carriers which had slipped out of the Kuriles on 26th November blasted the American Pacific Fleet as it lay at anchor in Pearl Harbor on the morning of Sunday, 7th December 1941. Eight battleships were sunk or badly damaged, and almost all America's air strength in the Central Pacific was put out of action. Guam fell on 10th December, Wake Island on 13th December. Hong Kong surrendered on Christmas Day. The Japanese landed on Luzon, the northernmost island of the Philippines, on 10th December, and took Manila, the capital, on 2nd January 1942. In a few months, the entire archipelago was in their hands, save for the garrison on Corregidor which held out until May. General Douglas MacArthur, commanding the forces in the Philippines, left for Darwin in Northern Australia

Left: Japanese troops celebrate the capture of the Philippines

117

on 11th March 1942. (Darwin itself had been bombed on 19th February.)

The advance was equally rapid in South-East Asia. More than two hours before the attack on Pearl, Japanese forces began landing on the east coast of Malaya. Others drove down the Isthmus of Kra from Siam. One regiment of the Imperial Guards was led in this assault by Colonel Iwakuro, who had negotiated with Bishop Walsh and Postmaster-General Walker in Washington only a few months before. Flying from bases in what was still officially French territory, Japanese bombers put paid to the ill-advised sortie of the British battleship *Prince of Wales* and the battle cruiser *Repulse,* unprotected from air attack, on 10th December 1941.

Using bicycles as well as lorries and tanks, three Japanese divisions converged on Singapore, driving before them a mixed and largely untrained army of British, Indian, and Australian troops. The impregnable fortress fell on 15th February 1942 after an entire division had been landed to reinforce the garrison. The commander-in-chief, Lieutenant-General Percival, had no alternative but to surrender. The city's water supply was in Japanese hands and he could not take the combined risk of street battles and plague on behalf of its civilian population. It was the greatest single defeat in the history of British arms, and it was inflicted by a numerically inferior force. There was more to come. The oil wells lay ahead, and in rapid succession the Japanese swarmed into Borneo on 16th December 1941, Sumatra on 14th February 1942, and Java on 1st March, annihilating en route an Allied fleet in the Battle of the Java Sea on 27th February 1942. Punching their way across the frontier from Siam, two Japanese divisions penetrated into Burma on 14th December 1941. Burma had entered Japanese plans only to the extent of the capture of Rangoon and some airfields in the south, but it proved amenable to the same lightning tactics that worked in Malaya. Rangoon fell on 8th March, Mandalay on 26th April 1942. The Japanese armies surged on towards India, accompanied by a mixed Burmese-Japanese force specially recruited for reconnaissance and political propaganda.

Japanese victories end the colonial era

For this was to be more than mere military conquest, more even than Japan's own economic salvation. It was a campaign of liberation for the colonial territories of East Asia, and the Japanese everywhere relied on help which their agents had ensured would be available from in-

Right: The bicycle at war: mobility was the key to the swift conquest of South-East Asia. Japanese forces head for Manila

digenous troops or civilians. Men who had spent months — sometimes years — in exile in Japan now appeared in Singapore, in Batavia, in Rangoon, hoping to set up governments under the aegis of Japan's 'Greater East Asia Co-Prosperity Sphere'. The former Burmese premier, Ba Maw, released from the gaol where the British had held him, was soon co-operating with the military government which promised him his country's independence. Into the ears of the dazed and bewildered prisoners-of-war assembled in Singapore's Farrar Park, a Sikh officer and a Japanese major spoke with passion of the new 'Indian National Army', which they were asked to join in order to fight alongside the Japanese to free India. The Indian flag had already been raised in the little Siamese border village of Hat Yai as the Japanese armies poised for their plunge into Malaya.

By the summer of 1942, Japan's navy controlled the entire Western Pacific, and, far across the Indian Ocean, had sent its aircraft to strike at the British fleet in Ceylon. Japanese soldiers on the northern shores of New Guinea were only 400 miles from the northernmost tip of Australia. Thousands of miles to the north-west her armies had marched to the borders of India.

No doubt the time would come when they would be forced back painfully, inch by inch, from these conquests. But meanwhile they ruled and, whatever happened later, their rule would ensure that the empires which the Western powers had set up in Asia would never rise again. Japan had come very far from the days of Perry and the British bombardment of Kagoshima — yet it had all taken place in a man's lifetime. Only twelve months before Japan unfolded her triumphant campaigns, the last of the *genrō* — Prince Saionji — had died. He was four years old when Perry forced his way into Uraga Bay and imposed terms on a humiliated *shōgun*. A year after his death, Japan was lord of most of Asia and half the vast Pacific. The Meiji Restoration was complete.

Top left: *General Percival, GOC Malaya (on right), marches out to surrender Singapore.* ***Bottom left:*** *Japanese troops on the border between Indo-China and Burma salute the rising sun*

Chronology of Events

1853   **14th July:** Perry anchors off Uraga in Edo Bay and delivers President Fillmore's letter addressed to the Emperor of Japan

1854   **13th February:** Perry returns to Edo Bay and secures the treaty of Kanagawa. Trading treaties with Britain, Russia, and the Netherlands follow

1860   First Japanese embassy to the USA exchanges treaty ratifications in Washington

1868   Combined attack by the Kyoto nobility and the armies of the southern clans displaces the last Tokugawa *shōgun* and restores Imperial rule. Emperor Mutsuhito takes the reign-name 'Meiji' ('Enlightened rule')

1868-1912   The Meiji Period: the anti-foreign policy is dropped, and rapid westernisation follows

1877   The Satsuma Rebellion: Saigō Takamori and his feudal warriors are crushed by the modern trained army of commoners

1885   The cabinet is reorganised on Prussian lines, Prince Itō becoming prime minister

1889   **11th February:** the new constitution is promulgated

1894   Great Britain accepts the jurisdiction of Japanese courts over British nationals with effect from 1899

1894-5   The Sino-Japanese war: the struggle for the control of Korea is ended by the Treaty of Shimonoseki

1902   **30th January:** the Anglo-Japanese alliance is signed

1904-5   The Russo-Japanese war: by the Treaty of Portsmouth (5th September) Russia acknowledges Japan's paramount interest in Korea, which is annexed by Japan in 1910

1912   **30th July:** Emperor Meiji dies and is succeeded by his son. The Taisho Period begins (1912-26)

1914   **23rd August:** Japan declares war on Germany, captures Tsingtao (7th November), and occupies a number of German islands in the Pacific

1915   **18th January:** Japan submits to China her Twenty-One Demands

1917   **2nd November:** by the Lansing-Ishii agreement, the USA recognises the special interests of Japan in China, and Japan reaffirms the Open Door policy in China

1921   The Washington Conference limits naval armaments

1926   The Shōwa ('Shining Peace') Period begins with Hirohito becoming Emperor

1930   **22nd April:** the London Treaty is signed

1931   **19th September:** the Mukden Incident — the Kwantung Army takes possession of Mukden in Manchuria

1932   Japan proclaims the independence of 'Manchukuo' (Manchuria) **15th May:** assassination of prime minister Inukai by military reactionaries marks the end of party government in Japan

1933   Japan withdraws from the League of Nations

1936   **26th February:** uprising of army officers in Tokyo

1937   **7th July:** outbreak of Sino-Japanese hostilities, which continue until 1945

1941   **17th October:** the cabinet of Prince Konoye resigns, and the pro-Axis General Tōjō becomes prime minister and minister of war

    7th December: Japan launches surprise attacks on Hawaii, the Philippines, Guam, Midway Island, Hong Kong, and Malaya

    8th December: the USA declares war on Japan

    25th December: British forces surrender Hong Kong

1942   **15th February:** Singapore surrenders to the Japanese

Top: Fukuzawa Yūkichi, a former samurai who became a leading advocate of Western ideas (left); a Europeanised Japanese sporting a hybrid style (centre); executed rebels, 1879 (right). Middle: Crown Prince Hirohito inspecting a Guard of Honour in London, 1921 (left); a pre-First World War American cartoon acknowledges the rising sun of the Japanese Empire (right). Bottom: Prince Konoye, who was succeeded as prime minister on the eve of war in 1941 (left); General Ueda, commander of the Kwantung Army in Manchukuo (centre); Japanese armoured cars in Shanghai, 1932 (right)

Index of main people, places, and events

Author's suggestions for further reading:

Meiji Restoration and the modernisation of Japan:
W.G.Beazley
The Modern History of Japan
London 1963
H.Borton
Japan's Modern Century
New York 1955
R.Storry
A History of Modern Japan
London 1960
C.Yanaga
Japan Since Perry
Connecticut 1966
R.Tsunoda, W.T. de Barry, D. Keene
Sources of the Japanese Tradition, Vol. 2
Columbia 1958

Social and economic:
G.C.Allen
A Short Economic History of Modern Japan
London 1965
C.Blacker
Japanese Enlightenment: the Writings of Fukuzawa Yukichi
London 1963
W.W.Lockwood
The Economic Development of Japan, 1868-1938
Princeton 1954
K.Shibusawa
Japanese Society in the Meiji Era
Tokyo 1958

Foreign relations:
W.G.Beazley
Great Britain and the Opening of Japan
London 1951
G.B.Sansom
The Western World and Japan
London 1950

Militarism and nationalism:
R.J.C.Butow
Tōjō and the Coming of the War
Princeton 1961
F.C.Jones
Japan's New Order in East Asia
London 1954
S.N.Ogata
Defiance in Manchuria
University of California Press 1964
R.Storry
The Double Patriots: A Study of Japanese Nationalism
London 1957
T.Yoshihashi
Conspiracy at Mukden: The Rise of the Japanese Military
Yale University Press 1963

Library of the 20th Century will include the following titles:

Russia in Revolt
David Floyd
The Second Reich
Harold Kurtz
The Anarchists
Roderick Kedward
Suffragettes International
Trevor Lloyd
War by Time-Table
A.J.P.Taylor
Death of a Generation
Alistair Horne
Suicide of the Empires
Alan Clark
Twilight of the Habsburgs
Z.A.B.Zeman
Early Aviation
Sir Robert Saundby
Birth of the Movies
D.J.Wenden
America Comes of Age
A.E.Campbell
Lenin's Russia
G.Katkov
The Weimar Republic
Sefton Delmer
Out of the Lion's Paw
Constantine Fitzgibbon
Japan: The Years of Triumph
Louis Allen
Communism Takes China
C.P.FitzGerald
Black and White in South Africa
G.H.Le May
Woodrow Wilson
R.H.Ferrell
France 1918-34
W.Knapp
France 1934-40
A.N.Wahl
Mussolini's Italy
Geoffrey Warner
The Little Dictators
A.Polonsky
Viva Zapata
L.Bethell
The World Depression
Malcolm Falkus
Stalin's Russia
A.Nove
The Brutal Reich
Donald Watt
The Spanish Civil War
Raymond Carr
Munich: Czech Tragedy
K.G.Robbins

Louis Allen is Senior Lecturer in French at the University of Durham. He has edited and translated several books by French and Japanese authors, including a translation of *Prisoner of the British* by Y.Aida, which concerns the effects of the Second World War and its aftermath on Burma. He regularly contributes articles and reviews on Japanese history and literature to the British and American press, and is currently preparing a book written from the Japanese point of view about the final, decisive battle of the Burma campaign.

JM Roberts, General Editor of the *Macdonald Library of the 20th Century*, is Fellow and Tutor in Modern History at Merton College, Oxford. He was also General Editor of Purnell's *History of the 20th Century*, is Joint-Editor of the *English Historical Review,* and author of *Europe 1880-1945* in the Longman's History of Europe. He has been English Editor of the *Larousse Encyclopedia of Modern History,* has reviewed for *The Observer, New Statesman,* and *Spectator,* and given talks on the BBC.

Library of the 20th Century

Editor: Jonathan Martin
Executive Editor: Richard Johnson
Designed by: Brian Mayers/ Germano Facetti
Design: HCB Designs
Research: Evan Davies

Pictures selected from the following sources:

Associated Press 98 119
Black Star London 82 88 92 99 123
A.Brett-James 107
British Museum 9 12 46
Mary Evans Picture Library 37
C.Golding Collection 100
John Hilleson Agency 27 28 30 123
L'Illustration 18
Imperial War Museum 88 128
Japanese Embassy 4 10 14 16 40 41 43
Keystone Press London 103 106 112 120 122
Keystone Press Tokyo 6 18 19 57 73 86 122
Kyodo News Service 19 62
Library of Congress 60 69 70 91 123
Mansell Collection 59
Pictorial Press 95
Paul Popper 1 7 25 30 44 80 81 84 95 102
Radio Times Hulton 22 33 54 76 96 122 123
Snark International 20 48 54 79 103
Time-Life Inc 107
Ullstein 20
US Air Force 104
US Army 116
US Navy Dept 115 120
Vickers Ltd 64
World Health Organisation 59